The Notorious John Morrissey

The

Notorious
John Morrissey

How a Bare-Knuckle Brawler
Became a Congressman and
Founded Saratoga Race Course

JAMES C. NICHOLSON

K UNIVERSITY PRESS OF KENTUCKY

Copyright © 2016 by The University Press of Kentucky

Scholarly publisher for the Commonwealth,
serving Bellarmine University, Berea College, Centre College of
Kentucky, Eastern Kentucky University, The Filson Historical Society,
Georgetown College, Kentucky Historical Society, Kentucky State
University, Morehead State University, Murray State University,
Northern Kentucky University, Transylvania University, University of
Kentucky, University of Louisville, and Western Kentucky University.
All rights reserved.

Editorial and Sales Offices: The University Press of Kentucky
663 South Limestone Street, Lexington, Kentucky 40508-4008
www.kentuckypress.com

Cataloging-in-Publication data is available from the Library of
Congress.

ISBN 978-0-8131-6750-3 (hardcover : alk. paper)
ISBN 978-0-8131-6752-7 (pdf)
ISBN 978-0-8131-6754-1 (epub)

This book is printed on acid-free paper meeting
the requirements of the American National Standard
for Permanence in Paper for Printed Library Materials.

Manufactured in the United States of America.

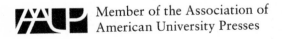 Member of the Association of
American University Presses

To Maegan

Contents

Introduction

Flags at New York's City Hall were lowered to half-staff, and the New York state senate adjourned to attend the funeral of John Morrissey in Troy, New York, on May 4, 1878. The *New York Times* reported, "No burial ever evoked so many expressions of sorrow from the mass of the people—the hard, rough working-men and women in the class out of which Morrissey sprang."[1] Fifteen thousand people stood in the rain to watch the procession as politicians, financiers, and sportsmen filled St. Peter's Church to pay their final respects to the man described in one obituary as "a prize-fighter, a gambler, a man without education or refinement, risen from the very bottom of the social heap."[2]

During his lifetime Morrissey was often maligned by journalists for his involvement in uncivilized endeavors. An American champion prizefighter, he was criticized for his participation in that savage art. He rose through New York political ranks to become a United States congressman and New York state senator but was condemned for having started his ascent to power as a street-level "shoulder-hitter," wrangling votes and intimidating voters for Democratic candidates. Morrissey's casino interests and Wall Street speculation made him, at times, a very wealthy man, a personification of a certain strand of the American Dream, but he was never fully accepted into the upper reaches of New York society. From the 1850s until his death he was involved in some of America's most important sporting events as an athlete, a promoter, and a proprietor, and his work helped lay a foundation for the multibillion-dollar American sports industry that would emerge in the twentieth century. But his most significant contribution to American sports, and his lasting legacy, was his role in founding Saratoga Race Course in 1863.

Despite being primarily responsible for establishing what has become the premier Thoroughbred race meet—and the oldest major sports venue—in America, Morrissey has scarcely been acknowledged, much less embraced, as a founding father of modern American horse racing. Presumably the hesitance to celebrate Morrissey's legacy is related to the reluctance of many to accept Morrissey during his own lifetime, when his association with the unsavory characters and practices of gangland New York made him unwelcome in certain circles.

John Morrissey did not learn to read until his teenage years and did not leave a broad paper trail. But we are left with an extensive journalistic record of the major events that helped to create his much-maligned public persona, which, by acknowledging his past, and attempting to convince the public that he was a changed man, Morrissey eventually used to his advantage, both as a politician and as a sportsman. His fame and notoriety helped Morrissey to attract attention to the early race meets he organized at Saratoga and helped him to keep cheaters, frauds, and other ne'er-do-wells away from the grounds; this, in turn, earned plaudits from a national press that was often critical of the sport of horse racing, which had been essentially moribund when Morrissey entered the racing business at the height of the Civil War.

Sportswriter Red Smith supposedly once explained that to get to Saratoga Race Course, one had to turn onto Union Avenue and go back a hundred years. There is a nearly tangible connection to the past, a hazy shroud of history and legend, at Saratoga. Part of that connection is attributable to the fact that horsemen, gamblers, and racing aficionados have gathered there for over a century and a half to participate in a sport that has been essentially unaltered by time. But there is an additional, unquantifiable element that attracts devotees to Saratoga, much of which can be traced to John Morrissey, whose fame and notoriety became attached to the racetrack as part of its unspoken foundational mythology and lore.

The colorful story of Morrissey's ascent sheds light on the intersection of gambling, politics, and tourism that gave rise to Thoroughbred racing at Saratoga and reshaped commercialized sports in America more broadly. Morrissey's ability to transcend and exploit his checkered reputation could serve as an example for the modern Thoroughbred industry at a time when a sizable portion of the American racing community continues to suffer the consequences of an inability or unwillingness to acknowledge problems with its own public image.

1

Wharf Rat

Like so many Americans of his generation, John Morrissey came from Ireland to the United States as a young child. A harsh combination of crop failures, a rising population, and civil unrest ravaged much of County Tipperary at the time of Morrissey's birth there, in 1831, causing thousands to flee to Canada and the United States in the pre-Famine years. Among the emigrants were Timothy and Julia Morrissey and their children, who settled in Troy, New York, when John was a young child. Troy's position on the Hudson River, near the eastern terminus of the recently completed Erie Canal, facilitated lively shipping and manufacturing businesses there and attracted many Irish immigrants to the region. Timothy Morrissey was able to find steady, though not terribly remunerative, work as a day laborer, and the family moved often, renting a series of shoddy dwellings in the area. John attended common school only briefly, learning "more mischief than letters," before being sent to work as a preteen in order to help support the family, which by then included seven sisters and a mother who struggled with alcohol addiction.[1]

In his early teens John Morrissey worked in a wallpaper factory, at an ironworks, and at a foundry, where he helped to produce bombshells for the U.S. military's use in the Mexican War, which opened up vast new territory for American settlement during a period of enthusiastic imperial expansion. At sixteen John took a job as a barkeeper and bouncer in a Troy tavern, where the young man received a valuable education in the ways of the world.[2]

Recreational fighting occupied much of Morrissey's time when he was not at work, and he won some acclaim in a series of impromptu scuffles, including a long rough-and-tumble fight that erupted following a local baseball game in which he soundly beat a notorious bully from nearby Albany. Morrissey's employer at the tavern, Alec Hamilton, witnessed the brawl and heaped praise on John, who was earning a reputation as one of the better fighters in the area. But Morrissey's fighting proclivities did occasionally get him in trouble, and around this time he served a few months in jail for assault and battery as a result of his part in a Troy street fight.[3] "I was the only boy in a family of eight, and had to support the girls," Morrissey later recalled. "I looked around me, very poor and very illiterate, and asked what I could do best of anything to get on. There was nothing I could think of but to fight."[4]

By his late teens Morrissey was one of the most infamous street toughs in Troy. In his words, he was the "chief devil" of a gang called the Downtowns. Predictably, the Downtowns' principal rival was a band of thugs called the Uptowns, led by a twenty-four-year-old derelict named John O'Rourke, who was regionally renowned for his fighting prowess. One autumn night Morrissey encountered a "partially intoxicated" O'Rourke, who was "in a quarrelsome state of mind," in a public square downtown. O'Rourke slugged Morrissey, and a brief scuffle ensued before the pair could be separated. Days later the pair again crossed paths, this time in a Troy saloon, and each was accompanied by his gang. O'Rourke again attacked Morrissey, who was prepared for the assault and soundly beat his assailant, earning hero's honors around lower Troy. In the ensuing months Morrissey would fight and defeat each of O'Rourke's comrades, one by one, further enhancing his stature with each triumph.[5]

That year, on a trip to New York City, Morrissey's tavern-owning employer, Hamilton, found himself in a barroom quarrel with a man named "Dutch Charley" Duane, who was a friend of American boxing champion Tom "Young America" Hyer's and a more-than-capable rough-and-tumble fighter in his own right. Hamilton told Duane that he had a bartender in Troy who could beat him, a claim that elicited only a laugh from the brawny brawler. When Hamilton returned to Troy, he told Morrissey about his encounter, and the young fighter made a mental note to find Charley someday and make him sorry for doubting his abilities.[6] That winter, rumors of a possible championship bout between champion Tom Hyer and challenger "Yankee" Sullivan "excited more interest than any other pugilistic encounter that ever took place in this country." Hyer had laid claim to the title of Champion of America some eight years earlier with a 101-round victory over "Country" McCleester. The American Hyer was a popular hero to the native-born in an era when an anti-immigrant movement was gaining momentum in New York. "Yankee" Sullivan was born in Ireland but had traveled the world under various aliases, staying the proverbial one step ahead of the law as he gained fame and notoriety as a fighter.[7]

State laws and local ordinances banned prizefighting across the United States, so a major part of the challenge of staging a high-stakes boxing match was finding a site that was reasonably accessible for gamblers without attracting the attention of the police. When the pair finally met in the ring on the Eastern Shore of Maryland in February 1849, a record stake of $10,000 was on the line. The parties had selected a secluded location, but in their effort to steer clear of law enforcement they had managed to evade many fans as well, so when the fight began there was only a scattering of spectators.[8] By the time the boxers staggered to the line for the sixteenth round, Sullivan had sustained a "slightly fractured skull" and could scarcely stand.[9] Hyer finished him off with a "blow on the face, which lifted him entirely off of his feet.

Tom Hyer successfully defended his American championship in Kent County, Maryland, on February 17, 1849, against Yankee Sullivan. Published descriptions of the fight spread across the nation, helping to broaden the popularity of an illegal sport. Years later John Morrissey acknowledged that he was inspired to become a prizefighter by the fame and notoriety that fighters like Hyer and Sullivan had achieved. "The Great Fight—Tom Hyer & Yankee Sullivan for $10,000," *New York Illustrated Times*, c. 1849.

He fell to the ground, striking his head severely—like a sack of sand—and was picked up by his seconds in a state of insensibility and completely blinded by blood, his face presenting the appearance of a butcher's block."[10] Hyer's victory, and the coverage it received in newspapers across the country, helped prizefighting gain broader popularity in the United States and produced the first consensus American champion boxer.[11]

Having already tasted the fame associated with pugilistic achievement in his hometown, Morrissey was particularly excited by the news of the championship fight, which only heightened his ambition to become a prizefighter.[12] That winter, a barroom brawl with a drunken belligerent landed Morrissey in jail, but his toughness had impressed a bystander, who paid Morrissey's bail and told him to go see noted political operative Isaiah Rynders if he was ever in New York.[13] Morrissey had just such an opportunity the following autumn while working as a deckhand on the steamboat *Empire* for Levi Smith, who would later become his father-in-law. The boat carried travelers between New York City and Albany, and Morrissey made decent wages, earning fifteen dollars per month, plus tips for delivering packages and luggage—a lucrative enterprise in the days before express shipping services.

Isaiah Rynders was born in upstate New York at the dawn of the nineteenth century and from a young age worked on riverboats on the Hudson, first as a lowly crewmember and later as the commander of his own ships, eventually earning the informal title "Captain." After accumulating some gambling debt in the early 1830s, he fled to New Orleans, embarking on a series of adventures in which his fame as a swashbuckler grew with each deadly scrape he survived. In one eventful trip down the Mississippi, Rynders quelled a mutiny and fended off a band of river pirates. In Natchez, Mississippi, he killed a man in a knife fight that started with a dispute over a card game, causing him to flee to South Carolina, where he oversaw a prominent horse-racing stable.[14]

Following the financial Panic of 1837, which brought much of the nascent American national economy to a grinding halt, Rynders settled in New York City, where he operated a series of saloons and provided protection for brothels and gambling dens. Soon he became an important operative within Tammany Hall, the New York political society with eighteenth-century roots that was a center of power for the local Democratic Party. In the 1840s Tammany's clout grew with support from the thousands of immigrants who were inundating the city, and Rynders controlled a team of "immigrant runners" who would help new arrivals find housing and jobs in exchange for political support. Soon Tammany Hall would become the major source of power behind a political machine that controlled New York City politics from the 1850s well into the twentieth century.[15]

By the late 1840s Captain Rynders was the de facto leader of New York's "Bloody Sixth" ward in lower Manhattan, which included the notorious Five Points district. Rynders gave orders to his henchmen from the headquarters of his Empire Club on Park Row near City Hall. He had founded the club in 1844 by enlisting a group of his sporting friends and muscle-bound acquaintances in support of Democratic presidential candidate James K. Polk. On the eve of the election, Rynders and the Empire Club led a parade of a thousand men through the streets of New York in an effort to boost voter turnout for the Democratic candidate, who had promised to annex Texas and pursue favorable terms with Great Britain over the border dispute in the Oregon Territory. On Election Day Rynders and his men used intimidation and violence to help ensure a Democratic victory. Polk carried New York by just 5,100 votes out of 486,000, and Rynders received broad acclaim from Democratic leaders, as well as a cushy appointment from Polk in the New York City Customhouse.[16]

The name Five Points was a reference to the five-way intersection at the center of the district that was, in the words of one historian, "a concentration of vice, disease, crowding, and bloody conflict unparalleled in American history." The neighborhood had once been a five-acre lake called "the collect," whose shores were dotted with butchers, tanners, and slaughterhouses. But as New York's population grew, the water became completely polluted, and the city filled in the lake, leaving an area known for its crowded tenements, noisy saloons, garbage-filled streets, prostitution, and extreme poverty. Few neighborhoods in the nineteenth-century world could have rivaled Five Points in terms of population density, violent crime, disease, and destitution. In the words of one publication, Five Points was "the most notorious precinct of moral leprosy in the city," a "perfect hotbed of physical and moral pestilence," and "a hell-mouth of infamy and woe."[17]

Morrissey later recalled that he was "very ambitious with very little opportunity" when he first came to New York. He knew that many of that city's famous fighters were members of Captain Rynders's inner circle, and Morrissey wanted to prove himself against the toughest men that he could find. So, he explained, "I took my bundle and came to the city, determined to get a fight out of them." He found Rynders at his Park Row headquarters. According to Morrissey's recollections, he approached the captain and calmly stated, "Mr. Rynders, I've come down here from Troy to fight. I've got no money, but I will fight for reputation. I will fight Mr. Hyer, or you, or anybody else you can pick out." In another account, Morrissey entered the barroom and demanded to see "Dutch Charley" Duane, the man who had scoffed at the claim that there was a Troy bartender who was tougher than he was.[18]

Like Morrissey, Duane was a native of Ireland's County Tipperary and had immigrated to upstate New York as a child. Duane had carried Tom Hyer into the ring on his shoulders for Hyer's championship fight with Yankee Sullivan and was himself an amateur boxer of some renown. (He acquired his nickname by defeating a German fighter called Dutch Charley and taking the man's moniker as his prize.) If Morrissey was looking to make a name for himself by defeating a famous opponent, Duane was a fine candidate. But, as Morrissey was told, Charley had gone to watch the horse races at the Union Course on Long Island.

Horse racing had been immensely popular in colonial New York, and there were at least seven racetracks operating in and around New York City as late as the 1760s. But in the aftermath of the American Revolution, racing was largely discouraged by patriotic leaders in an attempt to rid the new nation of vestiges of aristocracy. In 1802 the state of New York banned the sport altogether, though some rogues still managed to conduct clandestine races on a limited basis. Following the War of 1812, popular opposition to racing began to weaken, as supporters advocated the sport's capacity to promote agriculture and improve the quality of local horseflesh. In 1821 the New York state legislature authorized race meetings in Queens County, and New York enjoyed an early, if brief, golden age of horse racing, highlighted by a series of intersectional match races pitting the best runners from the North and the South, which drew huge crowds and heavy coverage from newspapers across the country.[19] But as the economic repercussions of the Panic of 1837 reverberated across the nation, New York racing declined precipitously, while the epicenter of American racing shifted to the south and west, mirroring the westward movement of American cotton production.

Attendance at the deteriorating New York racetracks fell, along with the value of bloodstock, as antigambling zealots continued to apply pressure to rid the state of what they believed was a contemptible sport. Opposition to gambling was certainly not unique to America, but the possibility of upward mobility in the United States in the mid-nineteenth century, which was comparatively unavailable in Europe, gave rise to a particular strain of antigambling sentiment in America that sought to protect social order, along with the myth of the American self-made man, against wealth and status created by means other than the kind of toil championed by the Protestant work ethic.[20]

A swan song for midcentury racing in New York was the last "great" North-South match race, between the aging "Queen of the Turf," a New Jersey–bred mare named Fashion, and the Alabama-bred mare Peytona, in 1845. Wild estimates of attendance at the Union Course ranged from fifty thousand to one hundred thousand, and a large band of toughs—led by Isaiah Rynders and including Yankee Sullivan—was enlisted to help keep order.[21] The southern mare Peytona proved to be too much for Fashion, winning two consecutive four-mile heats to take the $10,000 purse.

With the demise of top-class Thoroughbred racing on Long Island, the South's status as the center of American racing was secure, and it would remain so until the onset of the Civil War.

Regardless of whom Morrissey was nominally seeking when he entered Rynders's headquarters in the fall of 1849, the result of the visit was a severe thrashing for Morrissey: "They just all set on me at once, and give me a beating that made my head sore for three weeks," Morrissey later told a journalist. Morrissey held his own for a while and managed to keep his feet even as he was pummeled with clubs, bottles, and pitchers until he was finally knocked to the ground by "Big Tom" Burns wielding a ceramic spittoon. Morrissey vowed to exact revenge, telling his assailants, "Gentlemen, I will lick your crowd, and make you acknowledge me, if it takes me years."[22]

Although Morrissey had been severely beaten, Rynders was impressed by the young man's resilience. Rynders helped to bandage Morrissey's swollen head and put him to bed in an unoccupied room, allowing the young fighter to recuperate before heading back upriver. Despite his violent introduction, Morrissey was drawn to the city and, upon his return, soon found work as an immigrant runner on the New York docks, for powerbroker George "One-Eyed" Daley, during the flood of immigration that coincided with the Great Famine in Ireland. Morrissey would meet new arrivals at the harbor, help them to find lodging and jobs, and introduce them to the Democratic Party. "I was poor as a wharf rat, and could barely pick up my food," Morrissey later recalled, "but I kept on the wharves, unloading steamers, working with longshoremen, and getting beaten so often that I was hardly over right well." But Morrissey was winning his share of fights, too.[23]

The most famous of Morrissey's early New York City brawls became widely publicized only after his death. Tom McCann, a notorious rough-and-tumble fighter in gangland New York, had become jealous of Morrissey's budding reputation and, perhaps, of the friendliness between Morrissey and McCann's mistress, Kate Ridgely, who ran a brothel in the Five Points district. Mc-Cann and Morrissey met to settle their differences in a local saloon.[24] Early in their skirmish a stove was knocked over, spilling hot coals on the floor. McCann managed to pin Morrissey to the ground atop the red-hot coals, searing his flesh. Bystanders threw water on the coals, producing a great deal of steam, which distracted McCann. According to another version of the story, it was McCann, not Morrissey, who was scalded by a can of boiling water that was knocked from the stove. But the upshot of the tale is that Morrissey defeated the noted fighter and gained the nickname "Old Smoke" in the process.[25]

To supplement his immigrant-running activities, Morrissey found work as a card dealer at a gambling operation centered on the game of faro—a wildly popular fast-paced, luck-based card game with seventeenth-century French origins—in John Petrie's saloon on Church Street near the city hospital. There he learned the rudiments of the gambling business and how to turn a profit from roulette, cards, and dice. From that humble start, Morrissey would eventually become the most famous casino operator in America. In the meantime, he was familiarizing himself with New York's criminal underworld and continuing to make something of a name for himself as a street fighter.

Not satisfied with modest local fame, Morrissey sought the accolades and opportunities bestowed on top prizefighters. But, as he later recalled, "as long as I was poor nobody would do me the favor to fight me in the ring." Meanwhile, on the other side of the continent, the village of San Francisco had, seemingly overnight, blossomed into a cosmopolitan boomtown upon the discovery of gold in the Sierra Nevada foothills. Near the height of the gold rush, as breathless descriptions of fabulous fortunes to be made in the recently annexed California flowed back to New York, Morrissey set off for San Francisco, where, if he could not get rich, he might at least find someone to fight.[26]

With the completion of the first transcontinental railroad still nearly two decades away, there was no easy way to travel from one American coast to the other. The seaward option was by far the most attractive, but before the completion of the Panama Canal in the early twentieth century, that route included an overland portion across the Central American isthmus. Undeterred by a lack of funds with which to make the trip, Morrissey and his friend Daniel "Dad" Cunningham stowed away on a steamship bound for Chagres, in what is now Panama, as the vessel was being prepared for departure.

The stowaways hid among the steerage passengers for three days at sea before being discovered by officers collecting tickets. When the boys failed to produce proper documentation, they were brought to the captain's office, where John and Dad confessed to the unamused commander that they had little money. The captain furiously told the boys that they would be returned to New York and in the meantime would be forced to work in the coalbunkers.[27]

Upon the ship's arrival at Chagres, the principal port on the Atlantic side of the Panamanian isthmus, and before the captain could even release the anchors, a group of natives approached in canoes. That distraction allowed Cunningham and Morrissey to escape to shore undetected. They scrounged enough money to purchase tickets for passage on a boat up the Chagres River, but that trip still left them a hike of some twenty miles to Panama City, along the Camino de Cruces, a semipaved path built by the Spanish in early colonial times. Upon reaching the Pacific port town, the boys had only a few dollars left between them. Tickets to San Francisco cost hundreds of dollars, and they were being sold as quickly as they could be printed.[28]

After an abortive attempt to win enough for their fare at the card table, the boys hatched an alternative plan to gain access to a heavily guarded steamship anchored two miles offshore. They found a supply boat that was loaded with provisions for the San

Francisco–bound vessel. Marching alongside other crewmembers, they carried a large packing case onto the steamer and lost themselves in the crowd, hiding in the ship's bowels until they were well on their way to San Francisco. Again John and Dad ran afoul of the ship's captain, but they redeemed themselves by helping the officers to quell something of a mutiny organized by a conspiring cabal of rowdy passengers. Upon arrival in San Francisco, the boys located some acquaintances and borrowed money with which to repay the captain for their passage, but the seaman would not accept their offering. They instead used the money to start a faro game, which yielded enough to cover their expenses for the duration of their California stay.[29]

According to a colorful legend, Cunningham and Morrissey's maritime adventures continued, spurred by reports that had filtered into San Francisco of a discovery of gold in the Queen Charlotte Islands off the coast of British Columbia, more than one thousand miles from the Golden Gate. The boys joined with some nineteen other adventurers, pooled their money, purchased a small schooner, and hired a captain and first mate with promises to provide them a percentage of any profits the group might realize from prospecting or trade. They loaded the boat with food, water, and six small cannons, as well as one shotgun and two revolvers for each man. Perhaps because of their menacing cargo, the customhouse refused to grant the swashbucklers clearance to depart, so Morrissey and his cohorts waited for the first favorable night and snuck out of the harbor without papers.[30]

Their seafaring escapades yielded no gold but did include a confrontation with a swarm of canoes piloted by wary Haida natives, as well as an encounter with the HMS *Thetis,* an imposing British warship with a crew of over three hundred, at Vancouver Island. After joining the British officers for dinner aboard the *Thetis,* Morrissey and his mates departed for San Francisco under the cover of darkness, no doubt aware that they could have been hanged as pirates, as they were armed to the teeth in an area that was British territory under the 1846 Oregon Treaty. Upon their return to California, the comrades destroyed their schooner, leaving no physical trace of their adventure, from which the buccaneers were fortunate to have returned unscathed.[31]

During his time dealing cards to gold prospectors, Morrissey became acquainted with much of San Francisco's sporting crowd, and in the summer of 1852 some of those friends convinced him to challenge the champion of California, Scotsman George Thompson, to a boxing match. Morrissey had hoped to fight American champion Tom Hyer, who had come to California early in the gold rush, but Hyer had not remained there very long after drawing the ire of local law enforcement for his habit of entering saloons on horseback. So Thompson, who had been Hyer's trainer for his bout with Yankee Sullivan and had even mistakenly been arrested by police looking for Hyer the night before the fight, would have to suffice as an opponent, and the match was soon arranged, with Dutch Charley Duane, who had come west prior to Hyer's arrival, serving as a promoter.

Morrissey and Thompson each began five-week training and conditioning regimens surrounded by supporters. Some doubted whether Morrissey would stand any chance against the experienced champion. His public sparring exhibition in San Francisco, held a week before the fight, helped to convince some, but Morrissey was nevertheless the decided underdog in early betting. While he had a remarkable capacity to absorb punches, Morrissey was not an outstanding technical fighter, unlike the highly skilled Thompson. As the fight date approached, the local press publicized the match, playing up the ethnicity of each fighter—Anglo-American versus Irish American.[32]

Compared to its place within American culture more broadly, prizefighting was relatively popular in male-dominated California, fitting in well with the new state's wide-open culture. But even in California, boxing was conducted on the margin be-

Though he was never a technically skilled boxer, John Morrissey had remarkable strength and stamina. As one fighter later said, "You might as well hit a brick wall as hit that man on the head." Currier & Ives, 1860 (Library of Congress)

tween crime and sport. To attend a prizefight was to venture toward the fringe of civilized society. Therefore, as was the case on the East Coast, fights were held in semisecret locations, removed from public attention and scrutiny. The lively crowds at boxing matches tended to be composed of men who operated outside the confines of bourgeois society and included laborers, wanderers, assorted gamblers, and other nefarious characters.[33]

On the morning of August 31, 1852, a gaggle of fight fans gathered on the bustling wharves to board boats to Mare Island, a peninsula twenty-three miles northeast of San Francisco, where the Morrissey-Thompson fight would take place.[34] Drummers and bell ringers made a noisy racket as they tried to draw business toward the departing vessels, an indication that while fight organizers paid lip service to laws against prizefighting, they were probably not actually fooling anyone with their half-hearted clandestineness. Boat operators were charging ten dollars per passenger, a prohibitive fare for most people, though each vessel was equipped with musicians for the passengers' seagoing entertainment.

"The event created as much excitement as would the Derby in England," the sporting journal *Spirit of the Times* reported.[35] The wharves were decorated with streamers, and a large crowd of gawkers who had no plans to travel stood by to witness the spectacle. The decidedly pro-Morrissey assemblage of sportsmen departed San Francisco at eleven o'clock on an unusually warm morning and arrived at the shores of Mare Island around two that afternoon. Adding to the throng, a steamship arrived from Sacramento filled with boxing fans. Once everyone was safely ashore, a site for the fight was selected directly opposite the mainland city of Vallejo.[36]

At six feet one inch and weighing 178 pounds, the twenty-seven-year-old Thompson had an inch and a half and seven pounds on the twenty-one-year-old Morrissey. As the two were removing their overcoats and shirts just before the start of the match, a confident Thompson approached Morrissey and offered a $500 side bet (in addition to the $2,000-per-side stakes). Thompson had been the prohibitive favorite in the days and weeks leading up to the fight, but late support for Morrissey was growing, and some bets were taken ringside at even odds. "Well George," said Morrissey, "I've got no money, but I'll let you have what I can, and that's a good licking, so take off your clothes."[37]

The fight began with the boxers eyeing each other cautiously before Morrissey blocked Thompson's left-handed punch and landed a heavy blow to his midsection. The pair then clinched and toppled with Thompson on top. Under the London Prize Ring Rules first promulgated in 1838, throwing an opponent was permitted, but "hair-pulling, head-butting, eye-gouging, gut-kneeing, striking a fallen opponent, and blows below the belt" were not, and a fall by either fighter ended the round.[38]

As the fighters toed the line to start round two, Morrissey was laughing. Thompson threw another left, which was blocked by Morrissey, who landed a quick jab to his rival's head, drawing first blood, before a heavy exchange led to Morrissey being thrown to the ground. The third round began with "lively sparring," as Thompson landed a pair of body blows and connected with Morrissey's face. The shot to the head awakened the fighter, who then "went in like a Tiger, and sent home a corn-cracker on Thompson's knob." The pair clinched, and Thompson threw Morrissey, drawing cries of foul from Morrissey's corner, which the judges ignored.[39]

Morrissey was again laughing as he came to the scratch for round four and quickly landed a series of body blows, chasing Thompson to the edge of the ring. The pair clinched twice before Morrissey fell on Thompson to the audible approval of the crowd. The next two rounds were brief, each ending with Morrissey throwing Thompson, as the pro-Morrissey crowd continued to acquire confidence and evince enthusiasm. In round seven Morrissey landed a "tremendous feeler" on Thompson's chin before being thrown by his rival. Smiling as he toed the line for round eight, Morrissey "planted a lugger on Thompson's 'juggler'" before receiving a jab to the eye. With a surge of energy, Morrissey knocked Thompson to the edge of the ring, where

Thompson supported himself with one arm around the ropes as the pair remained clinched for half a minute. After they untangled themselves, Morrissey threw his opponent to the ground. Thompson rallied in the ninth round, landing a series of punishing body blows, but in the tenth Morrissey "made the claret fly" (drew blood) with a shot to Thompson's ear.[40]

In the eleventh round, after an exchange of shots to the midsection and a clinch, Thompson threw Morrissey. Jeers erupted from the Morrissey supporters, who alleged that their fighter had been struck by a low blow. The referee agreed and summarily ended the fight. Thompson's supporters were incensed and insisted that Morrissey's friends standing ringside had brandished weapons in an attempt to intimidate Thompson. Many witnesses claimed that Thompson had intentionally fouled Morrissey in order to end the match and escape with his life.[41]

Newspaper descriptions of the fight and the resultant controversy quickly made it the most famous sporting event in California, helping to cultivate interest in sports of all kinds there and ultimately leading to a gymnasium-construction boom in towns and mining camps across the state.[42] Emboldened by his victory in the much-publicized bout, and armed with the title of Champion of California, Morrissey returned to New York, a trip financed, according to one story, by a large bet on a horse race at Santa Barbara.[43]

The first order of business for Morrissey and his supporters upon returning east was to arrange a championship match with Tom Hyer, who was accumulating reasons to dislike Morrissey. In addition to being a champion in his own right, Hyer possessed a regal lineage within the world of early American boxing as his father, Jacob, had been widely recognized as the first American professional prizefighter. As a friend and trainee of George Thompson's, Tom Hyer was not pleased by Morrissey's recent victory, and he was not shy about verbalizing his unflattering opinions. Further, Hyer was an outspoken proponent of "nativism," a xenophobic and particularly anti-Irish and anti-Catholic movement that gained momentum in the 1840s and 1850s in the wake of a flood of European immigration to the United States.[44] Morrissey's controversial victory in California, combined with the fact that he was an Irish Catholic, would soon make him a conspicuous target of nativist ire and a hero to tens of thousands of Irish Americans in New York.

2

Fighter

Soon after arriving back in New York City, Morrissey sent a challenge to Tom Hyer. Rather than answer in the sporting press, Hyer delivered his response in person. Accompanied by Bill "the Butcher" Poole, a notorious street fighter, saloon owner, and Washington Market butcher (upon whom the character of Bill Cutting, played by Daniel Day-Lewis, in Martin Scorsese's *Gangs of New York* [2002] was loosely based), Hyer paid a midnight visit to Morrissey, who was asleep in his room above the Gem Saloon near the old Broadway Theater, and demanded to know why Morrissey wanted to fight him.

"Because you have ill-treated me," Morrissey replied.

"Get up and fight," Hyer demanded.

"You have got a friend with you," Morrissey noted. "Let me go and get one, and we will have a fight."

"I'll give you a show," Poole interposed.

"I have had a good many shows of that kind, and they make me sore," Morrissey replied as he ushered the intruders to the door. Morrissey was keen to fight, but not under those menacing circumstances.[1]

Not long after the midnight repartee, representatives of Morrissey and Hyer met at the Gem to discuss the specifics of a possible championship prizefight. As champion, it was Hyer's prerogative to name the stakes, but he had grown accustomed to the relative life of leisure that his fame had afforded him, and he was in no real hurry to return to prizefighting. Hyer insisted that any fight be for an unprecedented $10,000 per side, an amount Morrissey's group felt was prohibitively high, and the negotiations soon collapsed. Because Hyer remained effectively retired, the last fighter to lose to him claimed the American championship, so Morrissey turned his focus to securing a match with Yankee Sullivan.[2]

Although the press played up Sullivan's "Anglo" heritage, he was actually born near Cork, Ireland, in 1813. He had learned to fight as a youth and regularly found trouble in the British criminal underworld. In his mid-twenties he was sent to a penal colony in Botany Bay, Australia, and worked as a farm laborer there until he managed to stow away on an American-bound ship, arriving at Sag Harbor, Long Island, around 1840. He opened a rum shop in New York City but remained in America less than a year before sneaking back into England. He boldly placed an advertisement in a London sporting magazine seeking a prizefight and found a willing opponent in Hammer Lane, a talented English fighter. He defeated Lane, but only after breaking his opponent's arm, forcing him to fight one-handed. He earned the nickname "Yankee" by wearing an American flag into the ring in England and later returned to America to open another liquor shop while pursuing a boxing career. As one journalist explained, "Like many of the 'fighting men,' Sullivan had enough in him to make a smart man, but as it was, he was smart and shrewd only in a bad way."[3]

At a tense meeting in a Broadway saloon in the late summer of 1853, agents for Morrissey and Sullivan arranged a fight for $1,000 per side, to be held at Boston Corners, a tiny hamlet on the Harlem Railroad some one hundred miles north of New York City, near the borders of Massachusetts, New York, and Connecticut. The site was chosen for the ambiguous jurisdictional situation there. Multiple states claimed the area, and though in 1853 the site was technically in Massachusetts, it would be annexed by New York only four years later. Fight organizers believed that law enforcement would be less likely to interfere with a match held at Boston Corners than at any other site reasonably accessible from New York City.

On the morning of October 12, 1853, the *New York Daily Times* reported, "The trains of the Harlem [Rail] Road were densely crowded with hundreds of persons, whose curiosity was excited to such a pitch as to prompt them to abandon their business, families, and all else, for the purpose of witnessing the brutal exhibition in the ring."[4] Most of the crowd was composed of the lower-middle classes, as the very poor could not afford to make the trip and the very rich were not generally interested in the sport. The bettors took note of Morrissey's physical advantages over Sullivan and made him the solid early favorite. At five feet nine inches, Sullivan weighed only 154 pounds. And at forty-one years of age, he was nearly two decades older than Morrissey.

An old brickyard served as the backdrop for what the *New York Herald* called a "brutal scene, the particulars of which should make every animated piece of clay with a human heart in it shudder."[5] The fighters came to the scratch at 2:00 p.m., and Sullivan drew first blood with a shot to Morrissey's nose, to the delight of the crowd, which was estimated to be as large as five thousand. Sullivan had much the better of the early fighting, and by round four "Morrissey's face exhibited the most revolting appearance imaginable—his eye was dreadfully swollen and the blood was flowing in a perfect stream from each nostril." Morrissey's eye had been lanced to ease the swelling, but it was closing quickly, and his face was "shockingly mangled." In the process of inflicting damage on Morrissey's face, Sullivan had badly cut his left hand on Morrissey's tooth, severely reducing the effectiveness of his leading fist.[6]

By the sixth round, "although his face resembled a raw beef-steak" and "blood was streaming from his mouth in profusion," Morrissey "was as fresh and strong as at the start," and Sullivan was woozy from being knocked down in two consecutive rounds. But Yankee found a second wind and continued to pound Morrissey's nose and eye while employing a tactic of semi-intentional falls to avoid Morrissey's heavy blows. Under the London Prize Ring Rules, a fighter could not *intentionally* fall, but he could exaggerate the effects of a minor blow and take advantage of the thirty seconds of rest afforded a fallen fighter before the start of the next round. Sullivan used this rule to his advantage throughout the fight, landing quick shots to Morrissey's face and falling at the first opportunity.

As the boxers continued to bludgeon each other through rounds twenty and thirty, Sullivan displayed superior tactical skill, but each fighter had inflicted serious damage on the other. "Now, who's champion?" an emboldened Sullivan asked Morrissey, in a reference to Morrissey's supporters' attempts, in the weeks leading up to the fight, to have their boxer recognized as America's greatest. Morrissey, who had started the match as the betting favorite, was, by round thirty, the decided underdog in late action. By the end of round thirty-two, a witness reported, "it was a sickening sight to see Morrissey . . . the blood gushing in streams from nose, mouth, and half a dozen gashes on his face."[7]

In the penultimate, thirty-sixth round, "Sullivan went up to Morrissey, who appeared wild and weak in the legs, and struck him when and where he chose. His blows were not so forcible as at first, yet too much for human nature to endure much longer; and although Morrissey was bearing up manfully, proving himself as game a man as ever stood up in a ring, it was evidence that he was failing rapidly. His knees shook, and his hands were low, and his mind bewildered." Sullivan's "science and speed seemed about to carry the day" as the men flailed wildly at each other until they again tumbled to the ground with Morrissey on top.[8]

As the thirty-seventh round began, Sullivan continued his strategy of quick hits and dodges until Morrissey "at last succeeded in throwing his arm around Sullivan's neck and, getting his back against the ropes, lifted Sullivan entirely off the ground." At that point chaos descended on the ring as both fighters' supporters rushed in, and a melee ensued. The timekeeper, attempting to regain order, called for the thirty-eighth round to begin. Morrissey staggered to the line, but Sullivan, who had become engaged in fisticuffs with Morrissey's trainer, Orville "Awful" Gardner, failed to answer the bell.[9]

Under the London Rules, a fighter who failed to come to the center of the ring after thirty seconds was declared the loser. Morrissey's corner demanded a judgment from the referee, who ruled in Morrissey's favor, despite the fact that the fight should have been halted until the ring could be cleared. The fight was over, fifty-five minutes after it had started, but the controversy had only begun. As Morrissey made his way from the ring, Sullivan yelled after him, demanding that the bout continue.[10]

Sullivan supporters had reason to be frustrated by the decision, and a war of words was waged in New York City newspapers for weeks. By custom, the referee's decision was final, but many gamblers were reluctant to pay off on the estimated $200,000 of outstanding bets. Although Sullivan believed that he had been victimized by an unfair application of the rules, he did acknowledge Morrissey's uncanny ability to take a punch. "You might as well hit a brick wall as hit that man on the head," he conceded.[11]

Morrissey later called his fight with Sullivan "the hardest I ever had. He was an artist and he broke my nose and cut me all to pieces; but I have always known that I could keep my legs and stand up until any of my opponents were worn out."[12] The consensus in the newspapers was that Morrissey technically won the bout but had exposed himself as an inferior fighter, albeit one with an unmatched ability to absorb punches. "Morrissey is a slow man," a reporter for *Spirit of the Times* explained, "without much knowledge of ring fighting, and does not see advantages that others more experienced would take, relying more on his great strength and endurance than on science to carry him through. He is a game man, but a poor ring fighter."[13] Although not the most technically adept boxer, Morrissey would soon be generally recognized as American champion when Hyer refused to fight him on reasonable terms.

Reports of the Morrissey-Sullivan fight quickly spread across the country, but details were hazy at best and often completely false. A few newspapers even reported the death of one or both fighters. In a letter published in the local press, Morrissey addressed rumors of his demise. "Having seen a statement in the *Evening Day Book* that I was dead, I beg to inform you that such is not the fact," he wrote. A Cleveland, Ohio, editorial chirped: "It is to be hoped that the report as to Sullivan's death is true; it is a pity Morrissey was not killed also, as in prize fights and in duels, the best possible termination, so far as the good of society is concerned, is the death of both parties."[14]

The controversy over the outcome of the fight only added to boxing's growing popularity with the sporting crowd, but the sport remained repugnant to the more "respectable" classes, as evidenced by a *New York Times* editorial: "With the benefits of a diffused education; with a press strong in upholding the moral amenities of life; with a clergy devout, sincere and energetic in the discharge of their duties, and a public sentiment opposed to animal brutality in any shape, it is inexplicable, deplorable, [and] humiliating that an exhibition such as the contest between Morrissey and Sullivan could have occurred."[15] Law enforcement heeded the outcry, and Massachusetts authorities issued warrants for the arrests of both fighters. Sullivan and Morrissey were taken into custody in the weeks following the fight. Sullivan was apprehended by New York City police and extradited to Massachusetts, where he was jailed for a week before Tom Hyer raised his $1,500 bail. Morrissey appeared before a grand jury in Berkshire County but paid a $1,200 fine to avoid jail time. Warrants were even issued for the arrest of some of the New Yorkers who attended the fight, but enforcing laws against witnessing prizefighting proved exceedingly difficult, particularly after the fact, and the uproar eventually died down.[16]

The fame Morrissey received as a result of his victory over Sullivan could have been scarcely imaginable to him as a Troy youth. But a taste of success only fueled his aspiration for greater material wealth. The title of Champion of America would provide Morrissey with access to business opportunities and political power, but it would also prove to be an albatross in his later push toward social acceptance outside the Five Points, as he would be forever linked to a sport that many Americans believed to be barbaric.

Condescension from the "civilized" classes notwithstanding, Morrissey's increasingly recognizable name helped him to promote cockfights and card games and to attract business to the Leonard Street saloon called the Bella Union, in which he had acquired an interest. Meanwhile, Sullivan clung to his belief that he was the rightful winner and issued a challenge to Morrissey in the press. "It is entirely unnecessary for me to state that I fairly and undisputably was the winner of our last contest," he said. "But . . . I am willing to give the disputed money to any charitable institution . . . and make a new match to meet you again for $5,000, to come off within six weeks from this day. Man and money ready at my house."[17] Despite his pleas for a rematch, Sullivan never fought professionally again; he died a few years later in a San Francisco jail cell in an apparent suicide while awaiting deportation for election tampering. But Sullivan's controversial loss would soon be avenged by his friend Bill Poole, who had been a corner man for Sullivan in Yankee's fight with Morrissey.

The summer following his fight with Sullivan, Morrissey had still not been fully paid by the stakeholder, Jim Hughes.

Yankee Sullivan became American champion by default in 1851 and held the title until his controversial defeat at the hands of John Morrissey in 1853. Three years later he died in a San Francisco jail cell of an apparent suicide. (Library of Congress)

One night Morrissey found Hughes drinking with Poole at the barroom in the upscale City Hotel at the corner of Broadway and Howard Street, across from a saloon Poole operated called the Bank Exchange. Morrissey, accompanied by a number of friends, called out, "Hughes, are you going to give up that stake money?"

"I'll give it up when you convince me you won the fight, and not before," Hughes replied.

After Morrissey scoffed, Poole rose from his seat and, staring at Morrissey, stated firmly, "Hughes, don't you give it up to him; spend it for rum before you give it to that son of a bitch."[18]

Morrissey took exception to Poole's instructions and challenged him to fight. Poole responded that he would be more than happy to do so if Morrissey would first lose some weight. Morrissey then offered to bet Poole fifty dollars that Poole would not meet him the following morning at a place of Poole's choosing. Poole accepted the bet, naming the foot of Christopher Street, near his own home, as the meeting place.

Morrissey's friend objected on John's behalf, warning, "No, John, his gang will kill you if you go there." So Morrissey asked for another site. Poole replied, "How will the Amos Street dock suit you?" Morrissey agreed, despite the fact that the new location was just a block north of the first one.[19]

The next morning Poole traveled by boat to the wharf at the foot of Amos Street on the west side of Manhattan, arriving around 6:30 a.m. According to conflicting reports he had either been in Hoboken the night before in order to avoid arrest or had gone drinking with friends before the fight. Hundreds of gamblers, butchers, and thugs had already gathered and were exchanging bets. Poole told one ally that he felt "like a racehorse" as he waited for Morrissey. A few minutes later Morrissey appeared in a carriage at the corner of Amos and West Streets, on the banks of the Hudson River, and proceeded to the docks on foot after removing his coat and leaving it at a nearby store. He called for Poole as he navigated his way through the crowd.[20]

The fight began rather quickly, the conventions of an organized prizefight having been dispensed with in this informal rough-and-tumble bout. Morrissey threw the first punch, and the pair crashed to the ground following a clinch. The crowd of spectators closed around the fighters, making it difficult to tell exactly what was happening, but it was clear to everyone that Poole's supporters far outnumbered Morrissey's, and Morrissey received a severe thrashing before conceding. The whole affair lasted only five minutes. According to the *New York Times,* at the conclusion of the brawl "Poole jumped into his boat . . . and rowed away, while Morrissey, considerably chopfallen and awfully bruised and beaten, was obliged to leave the ground amid jeers and hootings of the assemblage." Poole and some of his compatriots spent the afternoon celebrating at Coney Island, while Morrissey was taken to the Bella Union to lick his wounds.[21]

The following day Morrissey's camp issued a statement to the *Times* that included a more detailed description of the encounter. According to Morrissey, half a dozen men had struck him early in the fight, and, once on the ground, he had feared for his life as Poole's friends kicked him while the Butcher was biting his cheek.[22] News of the fight, and of Morrissey's severe injuries, spread quickly across the country. A Massachusetts newspaper hyperbolically reported that, following the fight,

Morrissey presented a shocking spectacle, and scarcely could any of his friends recognize him. His eyes were closed, and one of them was found to be gouged from one end of the socket, which injury will probably impair his sight for life. His face above and below the eyes is blackened by violent blows given on the bridge of his nose. There is a hole in his cheek, and his lips are clawed up in a frightful manner. He also sustained fearful injuries about the breast, arms, and back, where Poole kicked him with heavy cowhide boots, after [Morrissey] had halloed "enough." So severe are Morrissey's injuries that it is very doubtful whether he walks in the street for the next six months.[23]

Morrissey did indeed receive a pummeling, but he recovered much more quickly than predicted. In fact, he was up and about the next day. As the *Times* explained, "All that troubles him are the bruises about his head and face, and the way he received them." But Morrissey was growing frustrated with the fighting life. His inability to convince Hyer to fight him was grating, and he had larger ambitions. "I desire to live peaceably and have the good opinion of all my fellow beings," Morrissey publicly declared. "I am no bully, and have never insulted a man first in all my life. I have lived in the City of New York six years, and never quarreled with any man except those fighters who seem to have a liking to hunt me out and cooperate together to beat me at any and every opportunity."[24]

His first step in furtherance of his desire to live peaceably was to marry his sweetheart, Susannah "Susie" Smith, the daughter of his former employer in his days on the Hudson River, Captain Levi Smith. Scarcely two weeks after his fight with Bill the Butcher, on August 10, 1854, the couple wed at her parents' Troy home in a double ceremony alongside her brother and his bride. Though by no means wealthy, the Smiths were far more financially comfortable than the Morrisseys; they were members of the Methodist Church and owned a nice house on River Street. Susie came from an old Protestant Yankee family, which placed her in a different social sphere from the immigrant working-class Morrisseys. Whereas John had not lasted a year in school, Susie was afforded an education typical of a mid-nineteenth-century middle-class girl. The wedding was attended by "a considerable variety, from the bootless, hatless dirty rag-picker to the 'finished gentleman,' while the street in front of the house was crowded by a motley assemblage of that exceedingly large fraternity of unfortunate individuals usually termed outsiders."[25] Susie would be described years later as "a large, impressive portly woman of good address and intelligence" and a "woman who attends the balls but has no social passion."[26] But in the meantime, following the couple's nuptials, she and her husband returned to the slums of Manhattan, far removed from balls or concerns about social passion. The couple lived on Hudson Street, and John turned his professional efforts toward his saloons and, during election season, street-level electioneering.

Between 1800 and 1850 New York City's population had increased nearly tenfold. Before 1830 migrants to the city had largely come from the American countryside and Protestant England. But in the middle third of the century new kinds of immigrants, especially Irish, flocked to New York. By midcentury half of the city's population was foreign-born. In certain parts of Manhattan that percentage was closer to three-fourths. Pressure on labor markets led to unemployment, which led to popular resentment of the immigrants, especially as the city increased its almshouse spending. The Irish were the poorest of the poor, making up 30 percent of the population of New York City but accounting for 50 percent of all arrests and 70 percent of charity recipients there. Widespread poverty helped to further depress wages, as hungry laborers were willing to work for anything they could get, to the consternation of the "native" working and middling classes.[27]

By the mid-1850s nativist frustrations had manifested themselves in the Know-Nothing movement and the American Party, whose leaders advocated removal of Catholics from public office, a twenty-one-year naturalization period, Bible reading in public schools, and a return to the "good old days" when early republican (Protestant) virtues had been bedrocks of a simpler and presumably more prosperous time. The combination of hostility toward immigrants and a tight labor market gave rise to an especially contentious election season in 1854. The fact that Tammany Hall was profiting politically from alliances with the immigrants made the Know-Nothings even more indignant.

That fall, Morrissey agreed to head a unit of Tammany's election team whose tasks included distributing ballots, herding

Fernando Wood served as mayor of New York City from 1855 to 1858 and from 1860 to 1862. Morrissey was an early supporter of Wood's and aided his first successful mayoral campaign as an Election Day vote wrangler. (Library of Congress)

friendly voters to the polls, discouraging opponents' voters, and monitoring polling stations for signs of chicanery (from the opposition). Specifically, Morrissey was assigned to provide Election Day muscle for Tammany's mayoral candidate, Fernando Wood, who, despite being a native-born Protestant and having once dabbled in nativist politics, had great appeal with Irish-born voters. Along with a squadron of henchmen taken from the ranks of the Dead Rabbits, a street gang composed largely of Irish immigrants, Morrissey successfully protected important polling stations from interference by the Bowery Boys, a nativist

gang led by Bill Poole. With the help of his Irish-American supporters, as well as some suspicious voting patterns that in certain precincts included more votes than voters, Wood won a slim
1,456-vote plurality.[28]

"With a majority of 17,366 votes against him, Mr. Wood
is mayor," one New York editorial griped. "Supported by none
but ignorant foreigners and the most degraded class of Americans, Mr. Wood is mayor. In spite of the most overwhelming
proofs that he is a base defrauder, Mr. Wood is mayor. Contrary
to every precedent in the allotment of honor through a municipal
history of nearly two hundred years, Mr. Wood is mayor. His as-
sertions to us that a murder by his own hands could not prevent
his election had reason in it. Fernando Wood is mayor."[29]

Born in Philadelphia in 1812, Wood was supposedly named
after the hero of a popular and lurid novel that his mother was
reading while pregnant. His family moved to New York while
Wood was still a child, and there, at the age of twenty, he opened
a wine and cigar shop, which failed after three years owing to
Wood's paying more attention to local political matters than to
his business. After a stint as a manager in a Virginia tobacco factory, Wood returned to New York in 1836 and opened another
shop. But he also joined the Tammany Society and quickly rose
through its junior ranks just as it was becoming a major political
force. Wood was elected to the United States Congress in 1840,
and, after an unsuccessful reelection bid, he entered the shipping
business. His ship *John W. Carter* was one of the first to reach
San Francisco in 1849, earning big gold-rush profits. He plowed
those proceeds into successful real estate ventures in San Francisco and New York, which allowed him to focus on his favorite
realm—politics.[30]

Following Woods's election, and under the tacit protection
of the new mayor, Morrissey was free to expand his gambling
operations. Although gambling houses were nominally illegal,
Morrissey was relatively unmolested by authorities thanks to

his political connections and the periodic donations to antigambling organizations made by Morrissey and his customers.[31] At Morrissey's gambling houses, patrons could play faro, as well as poker and roulette. Morrissey was also broadening his gambling activity to include a lottery game called "policy," a forerunner to what would later be called the "numbers racket," which would yield huge profits to Morrissey and his partners, including Mayor Woods's brother.

Morrissey would eventually become the most famous gambler and most powerful casino operator in New York. His gambling houses and policy racket were immensely profitable, but he had a long way to go before he would be accepted in social circles outside the sporting and gambling underworlds. A first step along those lines was to learn to read and write. He had gained only a rudimentary familiarity with his letters as a youth in Troy, and he saw that his lack of education might inhibit him in achieving his goals, so he allowed his wife to teach him.[32]

The couple's marriage was a mutually beneficial one, and John took his domestic responsibilities seriously. "I've played cards, and stood up in the ring, but I never let myself forget my domestic honor and duty," he told an interviewer years later. "It's the first thing to take care of all the days of your life."[33] Morrissey's marriage had a stabilizing effect on the fighter and was part of a general trend toward a more peaceful—if not always completely lawful—lifestyle. But he did not change his stripes immediately.

The gruesome fight on Amos Street between Morrissey and Bill Poole had only aggravated the discord between nativist and Irish factions of the New York City underworld, and Morrissey was eager to avenge his thrashing. Scarcely a month after his wedding, Morrissey, "somewhat under the influence of liquor," was arrested for barging into Poole's saloon looking to fight the proprietor. That winter, on Saturday, February 24, 1855, Morrissey again found himself in an altercation with Bill the Butcher.

Around 9:00 p.m. Morrissey was among a group eating, drinking, and singing in a back room at Stanwix Hall, a saloon on Broadway across from the fancy new Metropolitan Hotel, between Houston and Prince Streets. According to a witness, Morrissey left his table to confront Poole in the main barroom, where the Butcher was drinking with friends. Morrissey called Poole a "dirty cowardly son of a bitch," to which Poole responded, in reference to their fight on the wharf a few months earlier, "You had a taste of my mutton once, and did not like it."[34]

Morrissey shouted, "You dare not fight me with pistols over this counter."

Poole responded, "Yes I dare," before suggesting that they could even fight with firearms breast-to-breast as he produced a pistol from his pocket.

Undeterred by the weapon, Morrissey rushed at his rival, but the two were quickly separated. Moments later, a gang of Morrissey partisans charged into the barroom "as if they had been telegraphed." One handed Morrissey a gun, and Morrissey shouted across the crowd toward Poole: "Now you damned American son of a bitch, draw."

Both men brandished their weapons and pointed them as best they could toward each other, a difficult task given the number of bodies and heads that stood between them. Poole then yelled toward Morrissey, "Fire, you damned cowardly son of a bitch." Police summoned by the saloon owners arrived in time to witness Morrissey pull the trigger on his gun twice, with no result—misfire.[35]

Poole's friends shouted encouragement, but he ignored their suggestions that he fire his weapon. "No," Poole said. "I might shoot some innocent man, and I don't want to kill anybody. But let that big loafer get out from among them men and I will show him something." The police seized both Morrissey and Poole, taking the Butcher to the Eighth Ward station house before releasing him on a promise to behave. Officer John Rue detained

Morrissey, who promised to go home if the officer would join him for a drink along the way.[36] They stopped briefly at a small bar before proceeding to the City Hotel. According to the proprietor's testimony, when the pair entered at around 10:00 p.m., Morrissey was drunker than the barman had ever seen him. He was accompanied by Rue and three other men, including a pint-size thug named Patrick "Paudeen" McLaughlin, whose nose had been partially bitten off in a gangland scrape years earlier, and former policeman Lew Baker. Baker, an ally of Morrissey's in his Tammany electioneering operations, had, only weeks earlier, nearly been killed by Tom Hyer after Baker and his comrade Jim Turner encountered the former champion in the basement barroom below a Broadway theater. Not long after that, Poole had beaten Baker senseless in a Canal Street bar before police intervened, providing Baker with a motivation for revenge. After a brief discussion, Morrissey left the City Hotel, accompanied by Officer Rue. He convinced the policeman to make one more stop, at a bar on Canal Street, for a bottle of wine. There, Morrissey discussed the evening's events with a growing group of friends and allies.

Officer Rue left Morrissey around 11:00 p.m., on the promise that John would go home. Rue then went back to Stanwix Hall, where he declined a drink offered by Poole, who had returned to the scene of his earlier run-in with Morrissey. Dad Cunningham escorted a drunken Morrissey home around midnight, after two more stops for "one more drink." When they arrived back to Morrissey's home, which John and Susie were sharing with her father that winter while the captain readied a new riverboat, Levi Smith answered the door and helped Morrissey to bed.[37]

An hour later a group of Morrissey's friends, including Baker, McLaughlin, and Jim Turner, armed with pistols, entered Stanwix Hall, which had closed for the night. There they found Poole and some friends still drinking. Poole offered the men a drink, which was refused. Annoyed, Poole took one hundred dollars in gold from his pocket and declared that he could whip anyone in the room. Turning to McLaughlin, Poole told the slender gangster that he was excluded from the bet because "You ain't worth it."

An infuriated McLaughlin grabbed Poole by the collar and said, "You black muzzled son of a bitch, I want to fight you." Poole laughed, and McLaughlin spat in the Butcher's face. Poole escaped McLaughlin's grasp and retreated to the oyster box near the bar as Turner cried, "Boys, let's sail in," raising an oversize revolver above his head. With that, Baker, McLaughlin, and Turner advanced on Poole. Turner benched his gun on his left forearm and took aim at Poole some ten feet away but managed only to shoot himself near the left elbow. Poole raised his hands and said, "My God, have you come to murder me?" As Turner winced in pain from the self-inflicted wound, he again fired at Poole, hitting him above the right knee and causing him to stagger to the floor. Seizing the opportunity, Baker pounced on Poole and, after a brief tussle, shot him in the chest.[38]

Poole remained conscious for eleven days, and for a while it appeared as though he might recover, but on March 8 Bill the Butcher died from what the coroner confirmed was a bullet to the heart. The *New York Times* reported Poole's deathbed statements: "I think I am a goner. If I die, I die a true American; and what grieves me most is thinking that I've been murdered by a set of Irish—by Morrissey in particular." Poole's friends and supporters made sure that in death he was treated as a martyr by those who believed that immigrants, particularly the Irish, were responsible for the growing ills of New York society, including poverty, crime, disease, and moral decay. Just as they had hoped, Poole's murder became a rallying point for nativists; despite the fact that Bill the Butcher was a violent criminal, he was embraced by New Yorkers who felt that, in death, he reflected their experience by suffering at the hands of "foreigners."[39]

William "Bill the Butcher" Poole was a leader in New York's nativist gangland circles and the owner of a Washington Market butcher shop. He defeated John Morrissey in a rough-and-tumble fight on the Amos Street docks, and his death at the hands of Morrissey's associates the following year released a swell of anti-immigrant sentiment that was on display at Poole's funeral procession, one of the largest in the history of the city.

The crowd that packed the streets for Poole's funeral procession was the largest that had ever been seen in New York; estimates of its extent ran as high as 250,000. Even if the actual number were only a tenth of that figure, it would still have been a remarkable gathering for the parade, which included 155 carriages and 6,000 marchers. Following a service and an opportunity for friends to view the body at Poole's Christopher Street home, the memorial procession proceeded up Christopher to Bleeker Street and then down Broadway toward the South Ferry and Brooklyn's Greenwood Cemetery. Poole's casket was draped in an American flag, and a hearse drawn by four white horses was decorated with banners bearing his purported dying words: "I die a true American." The parade was led by a grand marshal and was accompanied by a fifty-two-piece band. Local politicians, fraternal organizations, and volunteer firemen and militias, as well as the recently formed Poole Associations of New York, Baltimore, and Philadelphia, joined the spectacle.[40]

Though many lauded him as an American hero, others found the martyrdom of a hardened criminal problematic. The *Brooklyn Eagle* declared, "The death of the bully Poole has been made the subject of a greater amount of contemptible humbug than was ever before inflicted on a community. [He was] but a knock-down, gouging, biting, brutal savage, whose end is quite in accordance with his previous life."[41] A New York minister also condemned the lionizing and reminded his flock that Poole "was no genius, no hero, no philanthropist, but he was a notorious fighting character. He kept a drinking and gambling house, [and] his associates were of the very dregs of society, men who live by corruption, violence, dicing, drabbing, and crimes that make poor human nature ashamed of itself."[42]

Despite such criticism, the story of Poole's murder and its aftermath continued to captivate the city for the remainder of the year, particularly after Lew Baker's flight from justice became front-page news. Weeks after the shooting, the *New York Tribune* reported that "the greatest excitement still prevails in the City, in relation to the murder of Poole and the escape of Baker; in fact, it seems to be about the only topic of conversation in every circle, wherever you may go." Baker had managed to sneak aboard the brig *Isabella Jewett* bound for the Canary Islands before Poole's death, but popular clamor convinced city officials to pursue him in a clipper ship called *Grapeshot*, which the city hired from shipping magnate George Law, a noted Know-Nothing who had made a fortune with his U.S. Mail Steamship Company during the gold rush. Despite the fugitive having a week's head start, New York law enforcement agents apprehended Baker off the coast of North Africa and returned him to Manhattan in custody. Baker's murder trial produced three hung juries and much journalistic fanfare, but not a conviction.[43]

Morrissey was charged with being an accessory to the murder, but the charges were eventually dismissed. A judge granting his release on $10,000 bail opined that there was "no evidence either before the coroner or grand jury justifying an indictment."[44] Five others, including Paudeen McLaughlin, were also charged. No convictions were ever obtained for Poole's murder, which some took to be proof that the criminal justice system had become corrupted by immigrant-friendly elements in New York City.[45]

As the hubbub surrounding Poole's death subsided, John and Susie Morrissey celebrated the birth of their only son, John Jr. Susie had returned to her hometown that spring in anticipation of the baby's arrival, and for a while John split time between Troy and his gambling, political, and saloon affairs in New York. As had his marriage, the birth of his son made a fundamental impact on Morrissey, and he vowed to become the kind of man that his son could be proud of.[46] Morrissey's seemingly genuine desire to stay on straighter and narrower paths could not keep him from occasional well-publicized brushes with the law over the next couple of years, however. In December 1855, the week of Christmas, Morrissey was arrested for threatening to fight Tom Hyer at the Lafayette Hall saloon on Broadway. The following summer Morrissey severely beat a man over a disagreement at a gaming table. Amid rumors that the men were planning to fight a duel to settle their differences, law enforcement agents, including Mayor Fernando Wood, were forced to intervene.

Up for reelection in the fall, Wood retained his office, by a plurality of the vote, with the help of a manipulated police force. He allowed supportive officers to ignore their duties during the campaign so that they might aid the reelection effort, and he furloughed part of the force on Election Day, which allowed his gangland allies more room with which to perform some of the electioneering stunts that Morrissey and his henchmen had pulled in Wood's previous mayoral election victory.[47] Months after the mayor's reelection, in May 1857, Morrissey was involved in a fight with waiters at the Girard House on Chambers Street at 7:00 a.m. Depending on whose version of events is to be believed, the fight began either as a dispute over a bill for breakfast (which apparently consisted largely of champagne) or as a disagreement over whether Morrissey should be allowed to sleep on the surface of the bar. Morrissey, who was accompanied by his faro partner

John Petrie, was reported to have been yelling with a knife in one hand and a gun in the other. A shot fired by Morrissey shattered the front window of the establishment, but no one was seriously injured. When the police arrived, Morrissey refused to be subdued and continued to wave his weapons menacingly as he attempted to escape. He was eventually apprehended and placed in the city jail colloquially known as "the Tombs." A friend somehow managed to post $5,000 bail—an illustration of the cash-flush circles in which John was by then traveling—but Morrissey was charged with felonious assault, and a popular clamor called for him to serve time for his antics.[48]

The day before his trial, Morrissey paid a visit to the district attorney, future New York mayor Oakey Hall, and begged to have his trial postponed. "I am here, Mr. Hall, powerless," Morrissey said. "Public opinion is hounding me unjustly. You can listen to it and send me to Sing Sing. But, bad as is my reputation, I beg for justice. In the present excited state of the community the jury will not weigh the evidence. I shall be sent to prison on my bad reputation and not on sworn statements." His pleas worked; the trial was pushed back, and Morrissey managed to avoid further incarceration.[49]

Later that summer, beginning on the Fourth of July, New York City became engulfed by a two-day melee involving hundreds of gang members, one of the most violent riots in the city's history. Named for the gang to which Morrissey had at least a loose affiliation, the Dead Rabbits Riot (also known as the Police Riot) grew out of a broader, politically charged New York City police conflict between the municipal and metropolitan police forces, the former friendly to Mayor Woods's administration and the latter run by the state. The conflict degenerated into a battle between rival gangs with opposing political affiliations in which eight died and dozens were wounded before peace was restored by the state militia. Though there is anecdotal evidence linking Morrissey to the riots, nothing stronger has survived.[50]

The Dead Rabbits Riot, named for the New York City gang with which John Morrissey was at least loosely affiliated, resulted in eight deaths and dozens of injuries before being quelled by New York state militia. "View from the 'Dead Rabbit' barricade in Bayard Street, taken at the height of the battle by our own artist, who, as spectator, was present at the fight," *Frank Leslie's Illustrated Newspaper,* July 18, 1857.

Lending credence to the belief that Morrissey was not directly involved in the Dead Rabbits Riot is the fact that Morrissey opened a saloon in Troy that year and took up residence along with his small family in a nearby dwelling for some respite from the turbulence of the city.[51] The following year, although he was not personally involved, Morrissey was the subject of an argument that resulted in the shooting death of Paudeen McLaughlin. During an intermission of a dancing session at William "Butt" Allen's Howard Street dance hall late on a Saturday night, Dad Cunningham overheard McLaughlin telling another saloon patron that Morrissey was "a big cowardly loafer" and a "goddamned son of a bitch."[52]

Dad grabbed Paudeen and said, "Don't talk that way about Mr. Morrissey—he is a friend of mine." Bystanders separated the two, and Paudeen offered to buy Dad a drink, which Dad declined.

"I'll meet you tomorrow and slap your face for you," Paudeen said.

"No you won't," Dad replied.

"I'll slap it now," Paudeen declared as he grabbed Dad's coat collar over the bar behind which Dad had retreated.

"Let go of me, or I will kill you," Dad warned. After repeating his warning, Dad shot Paudeen in the left breast with a revolver. Paudeen died two days later at the age of twenty-five, and Dad, who had turned himself in to police, was eventually acquitted of murder charges.[53]

As reports of street-level violence filled the city's newspapers, interest in organized boxing had never been greater. The summer before Paudeen's murder, three high-profile prizefights held in Canadian territory across Lake Erie from Buffalo, New York, had further increased the national visibility and popularity of boxing in America. One of the fights drew a crowd of six thousand, including both Morrissey and Tom Hyer, from across the northeastern United States. That fight, between two Irish saloon keepers from Philadelphia—one a Catholic, the other Protestant—lasted 152 rounds and nearly three hours, whetting the sporting crowd's appetite for Morrissey to return to the ring and defend his championship.[54]

3

Champion

Amid a surge in boxing popularity fueled by urban growth, the development of the sporting press, fight results transmitted by telegraph, and popular fighters' frequent sparring tours, a challenger to Morrissey's title emerged in John C. Heenan, who had gained a reputation as a fighter without ever having participated in a professional bout. Boxing fans, particularly those who felt that Morrissey was an undeserving champion, hoped that the twenty-three-year-old upstart would be a worthy opponent. Like Morrissey's family, Heenan's parents had come from Ireland's County Tipperary and settled in upstate New York. Heenan's father—like Morrissey's, named Timothy—worked as a foreman at the Watervliet Arsenal just across the Hudson River from Troy. Both families were of humble origins, but the Morrisseys were decidedly more working class than the Heenans. The families were familiar with each other, and a popular legend held that bad blood developed between Timothy Heenan and Timothy Morrissey as a result of a dispute over a cockfight.

Despite the similarities between Heenan and Morrissey, many fans placed great significance on the fact that Heenan had been born in the United States and Morrissey had not. Immigrants rallied behind the champion, while "native" Americans hoped that Heenan could reclaim the American title on behalf

Like Morrissey, John C. Heenan grew up in upstate New York. But Heenan's status as an American-born fighter made him popular with anti-immigrant nativists. "John C. Heenan, the champion of America," Currier & Ives, c. 1860.

of those born on U.S. soil. Heenan had worked menial jobs as a teenager in Troy (including, according to some stories, a stint as a coworker of Morrissey's at the ironworks) before moving to California in 1852. There he found a job in the Pacific Mail Steamship Company's workshop in Benicia. After an unsuccessful attempt at mining, Heenan worked as a political enforcer in San Francisco, where he became known for his fighting prowess. He left San Francisco when he found himself in hot water over some rough electioneering tactics and came to New York City, where some acquaintances in Tammany Hall helped him to procure a cushy job in the customs house. Friends, including former champion Tom Hyer, soon began promoting Heenan (whom they dubbed the "Benicia Boy") as a viable challenger to Morrissey. Heenan's supporters published a series of jabs at the champion in local newspapers, and boxing enthusiasts fanned the flames of conflict in hopes of a championship bout.[1]

As Morrissey later explained, he was at first none too keen to return to the ring, having given up that life in order to pursue business ventures. But he began to change his mind when, in his words, he was "set upon in and out of print, and finally they whipped my old father and abused my family. Said I to my wife, 'I can't live this way. I shall have to fight this man.'" Susie, who had first encouraged her husband to abandon boxing, agreed.[2]

Unlike Morrissey, who was already a famous figure in New York, Heenan was relatively unknown outside hardcore boxing circles. Thus fight promoters could massage his personal story to make him an attractive, "respectable" working-class alternative to Morrissey, who, in addition to having been born in Ireland, had a reputation sullied by involvement in crime, gambling, excessive drinking, and political chicanery. In the summer of 1858 Heenan published a formal challenge to Morrissey, which the champion accepted. The pair agreed to a fight in the fall for $5,000 ($2,500 per side), and each began training regimens that were followed closely by the sporting press.[3]

Morrissey remained in Troy for his fight preparation and used his father-in-law's land for some of his exercise sessions. His training days began at 5:00 a.m. with a beaten egg in a glass of sherry followed by a five-mile walk. He would then return to his makeshift gym at the Abbey Hotel near Albany to punch a sand-bag and work with dumbbells, followed by a massage, breakfast, and a nap. At 8:30 he would go for a ten-mile walk, followed by more weight training and sandbag punching, then another rub-down and lunch. In the afternoon there would be another walk, followed by sparring and a third massage. His suppers consist-ed of broiled chicken without seasoning, a slice of toast, and a cup of tea (water was generally avoided as it was believed to be difficult to work off). Evening sessions included rowing or more walking, a hundred-yard sprint, and a final rubdown before bed.[4]

Both men participated in a series of sparring exhibitions along the East Coast, which garnered additional publicity for the upcoming bout. Although prizefighting was still strictly against the law, the exhibitions were legal in many places, and quite pop-ular. The New York Clipper, a newspaper that catered to the sporting crowd, reported, "Fight! Fight! Go where you will, there is no other subject talked of but 'fight.'"[5]

Organizers agreed to make Buffalo, a booming port town on Lake Erie at the western terminus of the Erie Canal, the point of departure for a fight somewhere within Canadian jurisdic-tion. The exact location would remain a secret until the last mo-ment, in order to avoid interference from law enforcement. The gamblers, rogues, and sports that descended on Buffalo from as far away as New Orleans the week of the fight—including two known killers, Lew Baker and Dad Cunningham—turned the town into a scene evocative of the wild west and drew the ire of the sanctimonious newspaper reporters charged with describing the spectacle.

The New York Tribune called the crowd "the most vicious congregation of roughs that was ever witnessed in a Christian

City." *Frank Leslie's Illustrated Newspaper* explained that, while not all who traveled to Buffalo were violent men, "some of them are always ready with the pistol or the knife, which they do not scruple to use against any opponent who refuses to be converted to their own way of thinking."[6] The *New York Times* reported:

> It would be difficult to select a crowd in any part of the world whose features were more deeply seethed with every bad and foul passion that belongs to man. Indeed, did his Satanic Majesty desire to raise a special body-guard for state occasions he could not have sent his recruiting sergeant to more admirable grounds than Buffalo has presented the past few days. In all these saloons, crowds of these worthies were gathered on the night before the fight, all armed to the teeth with knives and pistols, playing the bully game and trying each to cower the opposing side. In one of the principal sporting saloons indeed pistols were freely presented, and it wanted but a little more rum to raise the row into another Bill Poole affair.[7]

Despite, or perhaps in part because of, this sort of journalistic disapproval, Americans eagerly awaited any bit of news about the fight and the spectacle that surrounded it. Back in New York City, as crowds huddled outside newspaper offices awaiting the fight results that were to be taken from ringside by carrier pigeon to a telegraph office, the saloons were open all night and betting business was brisk. An estimated $250,000 was riding on the bout in New York City alone, and heavy betting action was reported in Chicago, St. Louis, and New Orleans.[8]

Three steamships left the Buffalo wharves shortly before midnight on October 19, 1858. They were bound for Canada's Long Point, a sandy peninsula some seventy miles across Lake Erie. The tickets for these journeys were marked "excursion" or "picnic" in order for the travelers to maintain some degree of plausible deniability as to their involvement in the illegal activity. The first boat to depart was filled with Morrissey and his supporters, the second with neutrals, and the third with Heenan and his followers. A reporter for the *New York Tribune* cheekily described his unpleasant crossing aboard the "neutral" ship *Kaloolah*: "At 11:30 p.m. this floating coffin left the dock and steamed in a dismal manner up the lake. The crowd gave her a mournful cheer as she shoved off, and several persons on the shore who knew the boat, and had friends on board, bade them a sad farewell, and, weeping, turned away."[9]

The fleet reached anchor point, half a mile from shore, by daybreak, but the unloading of passengers and equipment by rowboat took nearly three hours, and many of the fight fans simply swam to shore. The ring was set up on a flat, sandy area in the shadow of a lighthouse. In compliance with the letter of the London Rules, which required that fights take place on turf, a few blades of grass were sprinkled inside the ring. As gamblers spiritedly exchanged last-minute bets, representatives of the two fighters selected a referee (after nearly two hours of negotiation) and appointed twenty-five "ring-keepers"—club-wielding thugs charged with preventing spectators' interference with the action inside the ropes.[10]

Morrissey supporters offered generous odds but insisted on enormous stakes. Morrissey himself even offered the Benicia Boy a large side bet, which Heenan had to decline because of a lack of funds. Despite Morrissey's decided disadvantage in size—some two inches and twenty pounds—his backers were confident. Not only did they trust their fighter's stamina and durability; they were also aware that Heenan had missed at least a week of training because of a severely infected abscess in his leg that had caused tremendous swelling and had still not completely healed.[11]

"Morrissey looked a magnificent animal," the *New York Times* reported, "red sinewy and lean. His eye, the index of physique, looked clear and bright, and full of savage resolution. Heenan, on the other hand, looked pale and dull of eye, and his

The championship bout between John Morrissey and John C. Heenan attracted thousands of spectators from across the nation and drew unprecedented attention from the American sporting press. "The Great Prize-Fight between Morrissey and the Benicia Boy at Long Point, Canada," *Frank Leslie's Illustrated Newspaper*, October 30, 1858.

muscles, though large, lacked consistency. He had a loose, boyish air about him, and he resembled an Illinois Hoosier rather than the firmer compactness of Morrissey. Altogether he looked soft, and scarcely cut out for a day's work."[12] Heenan's corner of the ring was decorated in red, white, and blue, and before the fight he wore a jacket lined with the American flag, which delighted his supporters.

As they exited their corners, the fighters were shirtless, and each wore white flannel knee-breeches. At 3:33 p.m. the men finally shook hands and began the fight for the championship of America. After some initial eyeing and pacing, Heenan made a right-handed feint from which Morrissey retreated, saying, "Not this time, my boy." They returned to their sparring before Morrissey took the offensive with three right-handed blows toward Heenan's head. One was blocked and the other two missed entirely. Heenan then countered with a right to Morrissey's eye and a left to his nose, which stunned the champion and drew first blood as cheers erupted from the greatly outnumbered Heenan supporters. Heenan pursued Morrissey to the ropes and unleashed a powerful left that missed Morrissey but connected with a stake supporting the ropes, severely injuring his third and fourth knuckles in the process. The fighters clinched, exchanging body blows, before Heenan threw Morrissey to the ground. Heenan's dominating performance in the opening round convinced any doubters that the Benicia Boy was indeed a legitimate contender for Morrissey's championship.[13]

After some initial feinting, the second round began with two blows from Heenan to Morrissey's nose and eye, "drawing claret." Morrissey blocked a third and followed with a series of shots to the Benicia Boy's ribs. Heenan got in another jab at Morrissey's face before the pair clinched and Morrissey was thrown to the ground. The third and fourth rounds included much of the same, with Heenan landing jabs to the face and Morrissey countering with body blows. Both rounds ended in clinches capped by Morrissey throwing Heenan to the ground. But in the fifth round, Heenan landed a vicious combination of a right to the eye and a left to the neck and jaw, knocking the champion to the ground "as if he had been kicked by a horse."[14]

When the fighters toed the line for the start of the sixth, Morrissey was "a fearful sight to behold—blood streaming from his face and head and spattered over all his dress." Heenan had only a bit of blood around his mouth but was visibly woozy, and his leg was beginning to bother him. They traded heavy punches, but both fighters were tiring. A witness reported, "Morrissey let fly with his right, but was cleverly stopped by Heenan, who followed up and got in three successive blows with his right and left on Morrissey's smeller, making the claret flow in a stream."[15] The round ended with Morrissey landing a shot to the ribs as he fell to the ground on top of Heenan.

Both men had to be encouraged by their supporters to make the start of the seventh round, but it was clear that Morrissey's superior stamina made him the likely victor. Heenan struggled to stand up straight as the fighters emerged from their corners, but the Benicia Boy continued to take shots at Morrissey's broken nose, and, after a weary exchange of body blows, the pair clinched and fell. With Heenan visibly declining, Morrissey was determined to end the fight in the eighth round. He went on the offensive, landing a series of punches to Heenan's midsection, but Heenan countered with more shots to Morrissey's nose and mouth, which Morrissey finally put to an end by throwing the tiring Heenan.

By this time both men were "gory from head to foot, a most sickening spectacle," according to the *Spirit of the Times*. "Both so weak they could scarcely lift their arms." In the ninth round, Morrissey drew Heenan toward the corner of the ring, where Heenan, flailing wildly, landed a shot to Morrissey's eye before the pair collapsed in a heap. In the tenth, penultimate round Heenan landed a few more jabs to Morrissey's face before missing wildly with a fierce right, spinning himself around and nearly falling down.[16]

In the final round, with both men nearing complete exhaustion, Heenan offered some feeble attempts at punches, each falling short of its target. He summoned the energy for one last looping shot at Morrissey's head, but that, too, missed as Heenan fell to the ground and fainted. His supporters carried him to his corner and tried to revive him for another round, but when time was called for the start of the twelfth, Morrissey staggered to the scratch, while Heenan was unable to stand. Heenan's seconds threw in the sponge, signaling defeat, and the referee declared Morrissey the winner as the champion's friends and backers rushed into the ring in celebration. The fight had lasted only twenty-one minutes, but it was immediately hailed as one of the greatest in the (limited) history of American boxing.[17]

Battered and bloody, Morrissey was too exhausted to speak. He attempted a smile, which was an ugly sight indeed. His eye was nearly swollen shut, he had cuts around his mouth, and his nose was bashed in, flattened against his face. Heenan, by comparison, looked relatively fresh. His lack of conditioning, which was at least partially attributable to the leg infection, had been Heenan's undoing, while Morrissey's remarkable stamina and ability to endure blow after blow had earned the champion the victory.

"He broke my nose and I think he could strike the most powerful blow of any man I ever saw," Morrissey would later recall. "But I won the battle."[18] When the warriors finally caught their breath, they were seated together in a carriage and paraded around the grounds to the satisfaction of the appreciative crowd. After some backslapping, continued drinking, and general celebration, the assemblage embarked on the return journey to Buffalo. Morrissey's boat announced their arrival by firing celebratory rockets, to the amusement of the assemblage on the wharves awaiting their return.

Descriptions of the fight filled New York papers even as publishers voiced their disapproval of the sport and the characters who supported it. Scathing descriptions of the scene at Long Point echoed earlier criticisms of the prefight crowds in Buffalo. "Probably no human eye will ever look upon so much rowdyism, villainy, scoundrelism, and boiled-down viciousness concentrated upon so small a place," the *New York Tribune* declared. "Scoundrels of every imaginable genus, every variety of every species, were there assembled; the characteristic rascalities of each were developed and displayed in all their devilish perfection." *Frank Leslie's Illustrated Newspaper* agreed, calling the crowd "low, filthy, brutal, bludgeon bearing scoundrels—the very class of men who have built up the Tammany Hall party in New York."[19] The *Times* crowed, "Of all foul breaths, never was fouler than that which made the dens of dissipation here reek with drunkenness and blasphemy the past few days, and made pestilent the air beneath the lighthouse of Long Point yesterday."[20]

The *Tribune* went on to expand its criticism of the sport of boxing more broadly: "The talk of establishing the Prize Ring in America, under an orderly supervision, is simply nonsense, judging from the people present at Long Point on Wednesday last. At present its patrons seem to be men who seek not to encourage a perfect development of physical strength and beauty, and an occasional good-tempered contest for mastery, but who only desire to gamble on the result of a fight between two fine animals."[21]

Despite criticism from the press, boxing had never been more popular, as evidenced by the swarms that had waited all night at newspaper offices for news of the fight. In the weeks following Morrissey's victory, crowds filled convention spaces to see the champion on his exhibition tour. Some newspaper readers complained about the broad coverage that the pugilists were receiving, but the editors who chose to publish fight news explained that they covered those stories in the same manner that they would a murder. Regardless of its objectionableness, it was news, they said.[22]

The sporting public immediately clamored for a rematch between Heenan and Morrissey. But they would be disappointed. A week after his victory over Heenan, Morrissey announced his retirement in the *New York Times*, explaining, "My duties to my family and myself require me to devote my fame and efforts to purposes more laudable and advantageous." He emphasized that he announced his departure from the prize ring not out of fear, but out of a desire to "more becomingly discharge my duties to family and society."[23]

Morrissey's first year of retirement was a difficult one for him and his family. Susie's father died in January, and she, John, and their son moved in with her widowed mother. Then, in November, Susie delivered the couple's second child, a boy, who lived only four days. While John distracted himself with his gambling pursuits in New York, Susie remained in Troy, periodically visiting the city.

With the money he made from the Heenan fight Morrissey began to build what would become a gambling empire. In 1859 he partnered with Matthias Danser in the established operator's gaming house on lower Broadway between Bond and Great Jones Streets, and later the two opened a gambling parlor on Ann Street. As he continued to profit, Morrissey expanded uptown with a casino at West Twenty-Fourth Street that was "elegant though not pretentious" and particularly popular with politicians and police. He also acquired an interest in an opulent den that catered to a more exclusive clientele, including bankers, brokers, merchants, and members of the "fancy" set, at 818 Broadway. There, patrons could read newspapers in the comfortably appointed lounge area, discuss business and politics, or engage in high-stakes gambling; the latter generated enormous revenues for Morrissey, who was becoming as renowned for his gaming houses as he had been for his boxing. In the absence of any real oversight, regulatory or otherwise, gambling dens were often operated by crooked and nefarious individuals. But Morrissey's games had the reputation of being played on the level, which made his houses especially popular with knowledgeable gamblers. Another reason for his solid reputation among the high rollers was Morrissey's promptness of payment, regardless of the size of the winnings. His casinos had secret vaults where the gamesters could store cash and hide their equipment in the event of a raid, but, given Morrissey's connections to the city's police and politicians, raids at his casinos were quite rare.[24]

With Morrissey retired from boxing, John C. Heenan became American champion by default, and he arranged a world championship fight (despite still never having won a professional bout) against Tom Sayers in England in the spring of 1860. Anticipation had never been higher for a professional match, and John Morrissey was among the throng of Americans who made the transatlantic journey to witness the event. Just before his departure, Morrissey learned some more sad news: his mother, who had battled problems with alcohol for years, was found dead in a creek bed in upstate New York, drowned while drunkenly trying to cross a bridge.[25]

Upon arrival in England, Morrissey publicly endorsed Sayers, the local champion, and appeared with him at the horse races at Newmarket. As Morrissey later explained, he sided with Sayers against Heenan because "by this time I was angry at years of persecution, and I wanted to see the last man of that old Hyer coterie closed out."[26] The much-ballyhooed fight between Sayers and Heenan took place in Farnborough, Hampshire, and ended in a draw after two hours and forty-two rounds. Police were forced to stop the bout when a mob of spectators rushed into the ring. At some point amid the confusion, someone pulled up the supporting stakes and the ring collapsed. A rumor that Morrissey was the culprit made its way across the Atlantic, but he vigorously denied any involvement.[27] Upon Heenan's return to the United States that summer, boxing fans begged for a championship rematch between Heenan and Morrissey. Several published rumors implied that the sides had started negotiations for a fight, but Morrissey was content to bask in the adulation he received as the most celebrated athlete in America. He was more interested in becoming the most successful casino operator in the world and would remain retired from the ring.

That fall, the presidential election was the topic of conversation across the country. New York City mayor Fernando Wood, who had been mentioned as a possible running mate for Jefferson Davis on the Southern Democratic ticket, bandied about the idea of a free city of New York, separate from New York State and the United States. "It would seem that a dissolution of the Federal Union is inevitable," Wood observed in an address to the city Board of Aldermen in January 1861. "Our government cannot be preserved by coercion or held together by force. With our aggrieved brethren of the slave states we have friendly relations and a common sympathy. We have not participated in the warfare upon their constitutional rights or upon their domestic institutions." New York City, Wood argued, could support itself on import tariffs and "could have the united support of the Southern States as well as the other states to whose interests and rights under the Constitution she has remained true."[28]

Nothing ultimately came of Woods's threats of secession, but they help to illustrate the state of flux that existed in New York and across the nation as America braced for war. Undeterred by the looming sectional hostilities, Morrissey set his sights on the fashionable resort town of Saratoga Springs in upstate New York, where his expanded gambling interests would eventually include a racetrack that would become a site of postwar national reconciliation.

4

Saratoga

By the time Morrissey opened his first gaming house in Saratoga, at the dawn of the Civil War, the region was already one of the most popular tourist destinations in America. According to local lore, the first European to visit the springs at Saratoga, nearly a century earlier, was Sir William Johnson, British superintendent of Indian affairs for the northern American colonies. In 1771 Johnson was still suffering from a wound that he had received in the French and Indian War at the Battle of Lake George. A group of Mohawks concerned about his condition transported Johnson some thirty miles, from his home outside Johnstown, New York, to a medicinal spring near what would later become the town of Saratoga Springs. The Indians built a hut for Johnson near one of the springs, where he stayed for four days. Johnson soaked his injured leg in the waters and, at the end of his stay, reported that he was nearly cured.[1]

Johnson was eager to spread the word of the curative properties of the Saratoga waters, and he wrote his friend Philip Schuyler to tell him about his miraculous recovery. Schuyler, an aristocrat from Albany, had a summer home a dozen miles from the mineral springs, near the Hudson River. In 1777 the house would be burned by the British during the Battle of Saratoga, but that American victory turned the tide of the Revolutionary War. At the conclusion of the war, Schuyler rebuilt his torched home and entertained many leading American political figures there, including George Washington, George Clinton, and Alexander Hamilton, who married Schuyler's daughter. Schuyler cut a path through the forest from the town (later renamed Schuylerville) near his house to the High Rock Spring in present-day Saratoga Springs.

In 1787 Alexander Bryan established a tavern near the spring to service the increasing number of early tourists in the area. Two years later Gideon Putnam, a Massachusetts-born miller, opened a sawmill nearby. Other settlers followed, and a nascent timber industry soon took hold in the foothills of the Adirondack Mountains. As the market became crowded, Putnam sought a more renewable revenue stream and purchased a small plot of land near Congress Spring (named in honor of the man who was credited with its "discovery," Congressman Nicholas Gilman from New Hampshire). There, Putnam hired builders to construct a guesthouse and tavern, which he called Putnam's Tavern and Boarding House. Others in the area called it Putnam's Folly because its size (three stories) and scale (room for seventy guests) seemed to far exceed any reasonable expectations for visitors in an area with only a few small cabins. But within a year of opening, he was ready to expand.[2]

Soon Putnam carved out walking paths around the spring and added a bathhouse. He bought additional acreage and began laying out plans for a village, starting with a wide central street that is now called Broadway, and he uncovered other springs and fitted them with pipes to make them more accessible for tourists. Within a few years Putnam had begun construction on a grand hotel he planned to call Congress Hall, but he was severely injured in a fall from some scaffolding in 1811 and died the following year from lingering maladies indirectly related to the accident. His children finished Congress Hall and expanded his guesthouse and tavern as an early tourist industry began to take shape.[3]

At that time, tourism at Saratoga existed in the shadow

of nearby Ballston Spa, which drew two thousand visitors each year to its fancy European-style hotel, with its backgammon and billiards parlors. In Saratoga, evangelist Billy J. Clark founded America's first temperance society in 1808, which helped give Saratoga an early reputation as a relatively pious place. Hotels hosted prayer meetings, and no guest could arrive or depart on a Sunday. But in 1819 the Village of Saratoga Springs achieved autonomy from the larger township of Saratoga, and local leaders ensured that both the pleasure seekers and the devout would be welcome. That summer Congress Hall added billiards tables, and it later introduced an orchestra for guests' evening entertainment. Countryside drives became a popular daytime activity, and gambling was tacitly tolerated in gentlemen's rooms. By 1825 hotels in Saratoga Springs could accommodate one thousand visitors per year, and a rivalry for regional supremacy with Ballston Spa began.

In 1823 John Clarke bought a patch of land in Saratoga Springs that included Congress Springs. He had been the proprietor of one of the first soda fountains in New York City and understood the potential commercial appeal of Saratoga spring water. He drained the swampy land around the spring and built a plant where he could bottle the mineral water. By 1830 he was bottling Saratoga spring water at a rate of a gallon per minute and shipping 1,200 bottles daily, promoting the water as therapeutic and invigorating. He employed dipper boys to dispense tastes, improved the walking paths in the area, and hired a band to entertain the summertime water samplers. Saratoga promoters sold the notion of the curative properties of the area's rural setting and healthful waters to urbanites, capitalizing on the fact that the region was then at the forefront of American culture, thanks to the work of writers and artists such as James Fenimore Cooper and the Hudson River School painters.

Saratoga was equidistant from New York City, Boston, and Montreal, and it proved to be a popular destination for affluent

Americans in an age of early industrialization, when many were concerned about the ill effects of city life, which included, in their minds, a seemingly endless wave of immigrants. And Saratoga had the added benefit of its association with a famous American battlefield, so it was a patriotic destination as well. Saratoga was promoted as a beacon of culture and civility within an idyllic rural setting. Every bit of justification for travel was needed to lure some reluctant travelers away from home, as many northerners, particularly those with a Calvinistic bent, were still relatively uncomfortable with the concept of leisure.[4]

By 1830 Saratoga Springs was drawing six thousand visitors each year, but travel to the area was still difficult. Steamboats had carried passengers from New York City to Albany for years, but that trip still left travelers with a rough stagecoach ride of nearly forty miles. In 1833 the Schenectady and Saratoga Railroad connected Saratoga to the Albany and Schenectady Railroad, the first in the state of New York and one of the first in America.[5] Saratoga promoter Gideon Davison, one of the founders of the Saratoga Railroad along with Congress Springs bottler John Clarke, observed: "A ride to the springs, which was formerly tardy and attended with clouds of dust and much fatigue and lassitude of body, now constitutes one of the greatest sources of novelty and pleasure in a visit to those celebrated fountains of health." By the end of the decade, Saratoga Springs was attracting twelve thousand guests per summer, and the increased accessibility of the region brought a broader spectrum of society.[6]

The wealthy and the middle classes regularly mingled at Saratoga, where a day's recreational activity often included a visit to the springs in the morning and a carriage ride in the afternoon. An English travel writer noted the relative lack of social stratification:

Hundreds who, in their own towns, could not find admittance into the circles of fashionable society . . . come to Saratoga where, at Congress Hall or the United States [Hotel], by the moderate payment of two dollars a day, they may be seated at the same table, and often side by side, with the first families of the country; promenade in the same piazza, lounge on the sofas in the same drawing room, and dance in the same quadrille with the most fashionable beaux and belles of the land; and thus, for the week or month they may stay at Saratoga, they enjoy all the advantages which their position would make inaccessible to them at home.[7]

Most of the entertainment options were completely benign; promenades up and down Broadway, veranda sitting, and eating tended to occupy a good portion of most travelers' days. But gambling, which had previously been confined to hotel rooms, was also increasingly, if gradually and informally, conducted in billiard halls and bowling alleys. Journalists' exaggeration of risqué doings at Saratoga sold newspapers and promoted the region as a tourist destination. As the number of visitors continued to rise, Saratoga hotels began to hire singers, dancers, comedians, ventriloquists, lecturers, and musicians in an attempt to lure and retain guests; a veritable who's who of the leading nineteenth-century American politicians, writers, and businessmen came to visit, including a handful of former and future U.S. presidents. Former New York City mayor Philip Hone described the scene at Saratoga in his diary during an 1839 stay: "All the world is here: politicians and dandies; cabinet ministers and ministers of the gospel; office-holders and office-seekers; humbuggers and humbugged; fortune-hunters and hunters of woodcock; anxious mothers and lovely daughters."[8]

In the 1840s and early 1850s, northerners and southerners relaxed together in Saratoga; black servants in the hotels made slaveholders from the South feel right at home, and many brought their slaves with them on their vacations. But by the late 1850s, as sectional tensions heightened, the number of southerners who traveled north to "take the waters" had declined appreciably, and by the beginning of the war travelers from the Deep South were rare. Wartime was perhaps not the most auspicious time to open a casino, but Morrissey established a gambling operation near the railroad station, in a large three-story brick building on Matilda Street (present-day Woodlawn Avenue) in time for the 1861 tourist season.

Gambling was still technically illegal, but Morrissey did everything he could to ingratiate himself to the town by donating to local churches and charities and buying municipal bonds. He assured anyone who would listen that women would not be allowed to gamble in his casino and that no locals would be allowed to patronize his establishment—only male out-of-towners would be parted from their money. His gaming house soon became nationally recognized for its elegance and was quite profitable. But he saw potential for growth despite the fact that the nation was neck deep in the bloodiest war ever fought on its soil.[9]

In July 1863 the Union army scored two of the Civil War's most significant victories at the Battles of Gettysburg and Vicksburg, setting the Confederacy on a path toward its ultimate demise. But less than two weeks after those monumental triumphs, mobs set New York City ablaze during the Draft Riots, the most destructive civil disturbance in New York history. The three-day bloodbath started as a protest against a federal law passed earlier in the year that created a draft, which amounted to forced conscription into the Union army for those whose numbers were drawn. Blacks were exempted, as was anyone able to pay a $300 commutation fee, which, the rioters felt, placed an unfair burden on poor whites. The protests began with stones and small fires, but the rioting mob grew in numbers and enthusiasm, and the scene turned into a full-fledged race riot as white protesters, angry that black Americans were exempt from the draft in a war that was increasingly being sold as a fight to end slavery, turned their rage toward black New Yorkers. More than a hundred people were killed in the New

York City revolt, and estimates of the number of wounded were as high as two thousand.[10]

Like the larger and more destructive riot in New York City, an uprising in Troy began as a protest of the draft but soon morphed into a violent antiwar and anti-Lincoln upheaval in which a number of blacks were beaten and stoned. On July 15, after rioters had destroyed the office of the *Troy Times* and had run off telegraph operators from their office, the mob attacked a Troy tavern and "demanded that the negro waiters should be given up to them." Morrissey, who was in Troy that week, told the rioters that the "negroes had all left but himself, and he was at their service if they desired."[11]

Before the violence, in the spring of 1863, Morrissey had announced plans to hold a series of Thoroughbred races in Saratoga that August, which, he correctly predicted, would bring additional tourists to the area and increase business at his casino. "All sections of the North and West, and some portions of the South, will be represented by their best horses, and Canada will also contend for some of the various purses," Morrissey promised in a published statement.[12] The *Saratoga Republican* evinced optimism for the endeavor and asserted that the races "promise to be among the most exciting and interesting that have taken place in the U.S. for several years . . . all the prominent turfmen are expected to be present."[13]

Saratoga had hosted organized racing before; a meet for trotters was first organized in 1847, and a reported five thousand patrons attended its opening day. A trotting track and a grandstand were constructed by two local businessmen and backed by the owner of the United States Hotel, James Marvin. Admission to the stand was one dollar for the good seats, fifty cents for the cheap seats. A ten-year-old mare named Lady Suffolk, one of the fastest trotters in history, won the first event of the meeting, adding to her remarkable record, which would eventually include victories in over half of her 161 career races.[14] Despite initial en-

Lady Suffolk, one of the most accomplished racers of the nineteenth century, won widespread adulation as the first trotter to complete a mile on a regulation course in two minutes thirty seconds. In 1847 she won the opening race at the first trotting meet at Saratoga. "Lady Suffolk, Centreville Course, L.I., Friday Aug. 3d, 1849," N. Currier, c. 1852. (Library of Congress)

thusiasm, the meet was discontinued after only a few years amid a steady decline in northeastern racing, which reached its nadir at the dawn of the Civil War.

By 1863 the stands constructed for the original trotting meet were dilapidated beyond use. With no place to sit, carriages lined the front stretch of the track, but trees and barns partially obscured spectators' views of the backstretch. Morrissey put up some $2,700 as prize money, which he quickly recouped in admission fees from the three thousand who attended the first day's races at one dollar per person. From the beginning, Morrissey envisioned his race meet as a national event. He hired Charles Wheatley, secretary of the Kentucky Association track in Lexington and former secretary to its vice president, John C. Breckinridge, to oversee the racing. As judges he brought in John Hunter of Westchester County, one of the leading breeders in the Northeast, and John Purdy, an amateur equestrian and wine dealer whose father had been one of the leading American riders of the early nineteenth century.[15]

As opening day neared, the *New York Times* conveyed enthusiasm for the upcoming meet. "This great Northern racing meeting, in which all the race horses outside the embrace of Dixie will contend, will commence next Monday, Aug. 3, and continue for four days. The visitors to Saratoga will have a rich treat, and, to the great credit of Mr. John Morrissey, the proprietor, gambling will not be permitted inside the Course."[16] One could reasonably wonder how many people actually believed that there would be no gambling at the racetrack, but Morrissey's willingness, perhaps eagerness, to pay lip service to the antigambling elements of society is telling. Talk of a crackdown certainly did not keep gamblers from flocking to Saratoga for the races, and Dr. Robert Underwood was ready for them.

Underwood, Irish by birth and a veterinarian by training, had settled in Lexington, Kentucky, where he established a veterinary practice and a racehorse training operation. But he would gain national fame by popularizing the auction pool method of gambling on horse races, to which he had been introduced in New Orleans by H. P. McGrath, who would later gain national fame as the owner of Aristides, the winner of the first Kentucky Derby, in 1875. Born in Woodford County, Kentucky, McGrath was trained as a tailor but learned the gambling trade in Lexington before setting out during the gold rush to California, where he ran a successful gambling operation. He later moved to New Orleans, where he owned one of the most lavish and profitable gaming houses in the city until the start of the Civil War forced its closure. From there he drifted to New York in order to capitalize on the large number of out-of-towners with expendable incomes who were drawn to the city during the war, and there he would later become a partner in Morrissey's Twenty-Fourth Street casino.

The Saturday before the racing was to begin at Saratoga, riders in racing silks paraded a string of horses in front of the

downtown hotels' verandas, helping to stoke the growing enthusiasm for the races among both men and women. That evening
Underwood conducted an auction pool at the United States Hotel for the meet's opening day. Under the auction pool method of
wagering, the auctioneer would sell the betting interest in each
horse in a given race to the highest bidder, thus creating a pool of
prize money. After the auctioneer deducted a small commission,
the auction proceeds would go to the person who had been the
highest bidder on the winning horse for each race.[17]

The first race of the historic 1863 meet was a best-of-three
series of one-mile heats for three-year-olds that was won by a filly named Lizzie W., who was ridden by a one-eyed former slave
named Sewell. Respected horseman William Bird, a free man of
color, trained the winner and would train all but one of the winners at the brief 1863 Saratoga meet.[18] The second and final event
of the day was a two-mile dash (a single heat) open to horses of
all ages. Morrissey entered his own horse, named John B. Davidson after his friend, which he had only recently purchased from
Kentucky breeder John Clay (son of the famous Kentucky states-
man Henry Clay). Despite Morrissey's promises that his meet
would draw the top runners from across America, the Civil War
had nearly decimated the American supply of available racehorses. So Morrissey had purchased Clay's talented colt in order to
bolster the ranks of equine contestants at Saratoga. Some observers suspected that the colt had been overexerted in his recent
workouts, and he appeared to be in less than top form as he approached the starting line. The other two starters were Thunder,
a sleek four-year-old gray horse owned by a Canadian, and a filly named Sympathy, who was Lizzie W.'s older sister. Morrissey
had secured the services of the top jockey in the country, Gilbert
Watson Patrick, a son of Irish immigrants who was known in
racing circles simply as "Gilpatrick," to ride his colt. Gilpatrick
had ridden in two of the wildly popular antebellum North-South
races and had guided the famous stallion Lexington to victory in

that horse's final race, but the celebrated jockey would lose by a neck to the filly in a close three-way finish to close out Saratoga's opening day.[19]

The start to the race meet received rave reviews from spectators and the press. "A large concourse of people included a host of the fashionable in carriages and tallyhos turned out to enjoy the sport and excitement," one local newspaper gushed. "Indeed Mr. Morrissey deserves great credit for the excellent manner in which the whole detail of his attractive entertainment is arranged."[20]

The second day of races saw attendance swell to five thousand persons, "the grounds being thick with carriages of every description."[21] The previous night at Dr. Underwood's auction pools, the gambling activity had grown commensurately. A horse named after John Hunt Morgan, the Confederate "raider" who spread fear and disruption through the upper South and Midwest, took the mile heats in the day's opening event. The second and final race of the day was a handicap (in which race officials assigned weights to be carried by the horses based on ability in an attempt to level the proverbial playing field). The man in charge of assigning the weights was H. P. McGrath, and he did his job well enough that bettors at the auction pools had difficulty deciding on a favorite among the horses. The jockey Sewell won for the second time in as many days, this time aboard a filly named Seven Oaks.[22]

The final day of the meet had been set aside by President Lincoln as a national day of thanksgiving for the recent Union military victories. He encouraged Americans to gather at their usual houses of worship, but that did not deter Saratoga's racing fans from heading to the track, and the largest crowd of the week saw the filly Sympathy defeat John Morgan in a pair of two-mile heats under the urging of jockey Gilpatrick. Her sister Lizzie W. concluded the meet just as she had begun it, with a victory, in a mile-and-a-quarter dash.

The *Spirit of the Times* gave the meet a glowing review: "By giving a great deal of money in purses, [Morrissey] secured fine sport. It is now established that of the many thousands of people to be found at Saratoga this season of the year, there are but few who will not eagerly avail themselves of the opportunity for such amusement and interest as the sports of the turf afford, [proving the] feasibility of making Saratoga one of the greatest places on the continent."[23] Attendance for the four days had exceeded all expectations, considering the wartime circumstances, and, as Morrissey had hoped, the meet had drastically increased business activity in town, particularly for the hotels and casinos. Morrissey made a nice profit by collecting admission to the races, but the real money, especially in the long term, was in making Saratoga a sporting center that would draw tourists and gamblers to Morrissey's casino. In order to build on that foundation, however, changes would have to be made.

Despite the profitability of Morrissey's 1863 meet, the racing facilities needed drastic improvements. Superintendent Charles Wheatley had done an admirable job under the circumstances, but the track's unusually tight turns, along with the absence of a functional grandstand, the obscured views, and the track's circumference being 297 yards short of an exact mile, practically necessitated building an entirely new racetrack. At the conclusion of the first meet, Morrissey sought financial backers to form an association to build the finest racing facility in America. "I saw," Morrissey later recalled, "that the racing stock of the South was nearly extinct, owing to the horses having been killed in the cavalry." Morrissey envisioned a time after the war when southerners would replenish their racing stock and return to Saratoga. He wanted to be able to capitalize on what he hoped would be a renaissance of American racing.[24]

Morrissey needed some well-connected and wealthy friends to put his plan into action, and none was wealthier or better connected than shipping tycoon Cornelius Vanderbilt. Morrissey had first become associated with Vanderbilt after losing a hefty sum of money in a speculation scheme hatched by some corrupt New York City officials in hopes of profiting from inside knowledge of the city council's intention to grant, and then revoke, a franchise that would allow the New York and Harlem Railroad to run a streetcar line down Broadway in New York City.[25]

Morrissey had lost as much as $80,000 in the failed plot, an indication of the immense amounts of money that came through his New York casinos and the connections he had forged in the city with wealthy and politically influential friends. He went to see Vanderbilt, whom he knew only slightly, at the Commodore's stables and found him preparing to go for a drive. Vanderbilt had quietly been acquiring shares in the stock that the plotters had tried to manipulate, and he had profited nicely at their expense. Morrissey assured the financier that he had not come to complain. Rather, he asked Vanderbilt for any stock tips that he would be willing to share in the future. Vanderbilt, impressed by Morrissey's boldness, encouraged him to come talk to him regularly and even offered to loan him $20,000 with which to begin the Saratoga gambling season. Morrissey took Vanderbilt up on his loan offer, and when he tried to give the Commodore a promissory note, Vanderbilt refused it, saying, "If your word is not good, your note is certainly of no account."[26]

Vanderbilt regularly visited Saratoga and, once their friendship had been established, frequently talked horses with Morrissey, who owned a trotter that Vanderbilt was keen to purchase. Morrissey had turned down $10,000 offers for the horse, and Vanderbilt asked him how much it would take to buy him. Morrissey again insisted that the horse was not for sale but told the Commodore that he would be happy if Vanderbilt would accept it as a gift. "Had I sold the horse to Mr. Vanderbilt for a round sum, he would at once have concluded that I had no gratitude, and merely desired his acquaintance for selfish purposes," Morrissey later explained.[27] Vanderbilt accepted the horse and kept Morrissey abreast of some of his stock ventures, from which

Cornelius Vanderbilt created a shipping and railroad empire that made him the wealthiest man in nineteenth-century America. Before their relationship soured, Vanderbilt helped John Morrissey to assemble the group that would open a state-of-the-art racing facility at Saratoga in 1864. (Library of Congress)

Morrissey realized some tidy profits over the next few years. Vanderbilt was one of the wealthiest men in the world and dealt notoriously harshly with people who crossed him, so Morrissey did well to put himself in Vanderbilt's good graces.[28]

At the conclusion of the 1863 meet, Vanderbilt helped Morrissey to organize a group of wealthy and prominent investors to build a state-of-the-art racetrack across the street from the old trotting track. William R. Travers, a New York City businessman, stockbroker, and member of some two dozen social clubs, was made president of the group, which would later be incorporated as the Saratoga Association for the Improvement of the Breed of Horses. New York legislation passed in 1854 allowed specifically for the formation of jockey clubs "for the improvement of the breed of horses." Presumably the association hoped that the inclusion of those magic words in its name would provide an additional buffer against antiracing and antigambling forces both within and outside government. According to the incorporating documents, "The Objects of said association shall be to improve the breed of horses; and for carrying out the objects of this act, the association may hold one or more meetings upon their grounds in each year, for the exhibition and trial of such animals as the directors may deem proper; and may offer and give such premiums as they may agree upon for superiority in the object sought for." In other words, this was an association created to conduct horse racing.[29]

Travers's partner in a successful investment firm, Leonard Jerome, was made a vice president of the Saratoga Association, along with John Purdy. Other members of the group included New York Central Railroad president and former congressman Erastus Corning; Vanderbilt's son-in-law George A. Osgood; Saratoga hotelier and recently elected congressman James Marvin; and John Davidson, a Hudson riverboat owner and namesake of Morrissey's horse. The association made local politician John H. White treasurer and named Charles Wheatley secretary.

Morrissey's name was conspicuously absent from the founding documents of the Saratoga Association, considering that it had been his idea and that he contributed more money to its initial capitalization than anyone else. Not surprisingly, there was some confusion as to the exact nature of Morrissey's roles in the racetrack and the company. As the 1863 meet came to a close, the *Spirit of the Times* said of Morrissey, "Much credit is due the lessee for the energy he displayed in the outset, in originating the plan of operation; but his only connection with the club, and the only one he desires, will be in an executive capacity." Another newspaper reported that Morrissey was "to be the Owner in Chief of the new and magnificent Saratoga race course." Historian Edward Hotaling eloquently summarized the situation: "As the new powers consigned [Morrissey] to official oblivion, they revealed, indirectly and doubtless unwittingly, what seemed obvious: that the whole idea had been his, and that his drive had pulled it off."[30]

Later that year an incident reported in the *New York Times* served as a good illustration of the reason Morrissey's name was excluded from the association's paper trail. On Christmas night Morrissey and his friends were drinking at Hoyt's barroom on Broadway in New York City. Morrissey was "under the influence of too liberal living during the day" and instigated a verbal altercation with a small-time politician and gambler named Andy Sheehan. The following night Morrissey was in Florence's bar at the corner of Houston and Broadway when Sheehan walked in and began a verbal assault. Morrissey told him, "This [is] no place for notoriety," and convinced him to step outside, where Sheehan punched him, starting a "terrific fight." The men were eventually separated by two police officers and taken to jail. The incident was not a particularly noteworthy one in Morrissey's life, but opponents of gambling and horse racing would have held it against the Saratoga organizers had Morrissey held a nominal position of leadership.[31]

The Saratoga Association, once called America's "first national sports organization," acquired seventy-one acres across the road from the old track, on the south side of East Congress Street (now Union Avenue), for around $7,000. The group also purchased twenty-three acres that included the former trotting track for $3,600, placing the association's landholdings at just under one hundred acres for what they envisioned as a world-class racing and training facility. They built a state-of-the-art grandstand and had the racetrack and grounds ready for racing the following summer. The *Times* reported that the association had made improvements to its new facility "without regard to cost. The grand stand or pavilion will compare favorably with many of the most famous in Europe; the track has been thoroughly laid and rolled, the fencing is perfect, and all the arrangements calculated to tickle 'the fancy,' and attract the attention of the millions."[32]

In July 1864 the association published an advertisement in New York City newspapers, signed by Travers and Wheatley: "The splendid new course is now completed, and is much admired by all who visit it. The stand accommodations are ample, affording a perfect view of the entire course from each seat. All the best horses in the country will be in attendance, and the most exciting trials of speed are anticipated. An efficient police will secure good order. Persons leaving New York in the evening can reach Saratoga at 9 o'clock [the] next morning. Extra trains will also leave Troy and Albany at 9 A.M. and arrive at Saratoga in time for the racing."[33]

On opening day for the new facility, the parade of carriages from downtown to the racetrack was well under way by midmorning. As had been Morrissey's policy at the old track, women were charged admission. Some thought this practice unseemly, but, in addition to padding the track's coffers, treating women as regular customers helped to legitimize their presence, and the large female contingent at Saratoga contributed to a festive atmosphere that was a vital aspect of the track's early appeal, helping

From the very first meet, women were welcome at the Saratoga races, and their presence helped convince sanctimonious skeptics that the racetrack was an acceptable place for even the socially prominent. "Our Watering Places—Horse-Racing at Saratoga," by Winslow Homer (1836–1910), *Harper's Weekly,* August 24, 1865.

to render the racetrack an acceptable destination and pastime for a broader range of society. In addition to the thousands of women in attendance, some of the wealthiest men in America showed up to have a first look at the new racecourse, including Commodore Vanderbilt, trailblazing retailer A. T. Stewart, and tobacco kingpin Pierre Lorillard, along with numerous leaders in sporting and political circles. The *Times* radiated praise for the new facilities. "Neither pains nor expense have been spared to render it perfect in all its departments. The spacious grand stand is a model of elegance, with its covered balconies, broad stairways, retiring and refreshment rooms, ladies' boudoirs and every needful convenience."[34]

The first and featured race of the day was the inaugural running of the Travers Stakes for three-year-old colts and fillies. Named for the association president, the Travers is now the old-

Upon its completion in 1864, the new racing facility at Saratoga was widely regarded as the best racecourse in the country. "The Saratoga Races—View of the Grand Stand—The Horses Starting," wood engraving from a photograph by Matthew Brady (1822–1896), *Frank Leslie's Illustrated Newspaper*, 1865.

est major race for three-year-old Thoroughbreds in the United States. One of the five starters in the first Travers Stakes was a bay colt named Kentucky, who had been purchased from his breeder, John Clay, as a two-year-old by John Purdy acting as an agent for a group of New Yorkers that included his fellow Saratoga executives John Hunter, William Travers, and George Osgood.

Kentucky had been undefeated before a loss in the Jersey Derby (the first "Derby" run in America) that June. He would ultimately win twenty-one races in a distinguished Hall of Fame career, but in the early betting on the first Travers Stakes, Kentucky was made third favorite, due in part to a report that he had appeared to be lame. Tipperary, owned and bred by H. P. McGrath, had finished ahead of Kentucky in the Jersey Derby, and the bettors made him the favorite in the auction pools. But Kentucky would have his way on the racetrack that day. Tipperary took a quick lead at the start, but Kentucky eased to the front of the field after a quarter mile. Kentucky's jockey, Gilpatrick, kept a tight hold of his horse until they reached the homestretch, when he turned the bay colt loose. Tipperary made a late challenge, but Kentucky held him off easily and won by four comfortable lengths.

Attendance increased throughout the week, and, after a record crowd on closing day, the *Times* declared that "the track henceforth will be regarded as the best racecourse in the country."[35] Morrissey, who had presided over the racing "with his broad shirt-collar flying loose, and streams of perspiration and dust forming miniature maps of the Mississippi down his cheeks, now betting, now giving instructions to policemen, and continually chewing on an unlit segar," had taken care to ensure that the opening meet at the new track ran smoothly.[36] In one instance he was proactive. As the *Times* explained, "When the season commenced, a crowd of thieves, three-card-monte men and their associates, came up and were landed at the depot. Mr. Morrissey, with several detectives, was on the lookout for them, and Morrissey, in a very quiet way, sent them all back. He said to them: 'Boys, I never interfere with your game—don't you interfere with mine; if you do, I will have every one of you sent to the Penitentiary for six months.' This timely advice sent the crowd back to New York again."[37]

Following the conclusion of the 1864 race meet at Saratoga, the association spent thousands of dollars expanding the grounds, planting trees, improving walkways, enlarging the grandstand to include some 4,500 cushioned and covered seats, improving stabling facilities at the training grounds, and adding a section of seating reserved for ladies. The return of racing was eagerly anticipated in Saratoga, and by the start of the 1865 tourist season, the Civil War had ended and thousands flocked to Saratoga Springs to join in the celebration. Morrissey decided to capitalize on the surge of patriotic enthusiasm by holding a series of trotting races two weeks before the Thoroughbred meet. While the races themselves were mediocre, a reporter for the *New York Times* declared that the meet

was conducted in an exceedingly genteel manner and was, there-fore, the more enjoyable by the large number of respectable families attending each race; not a boisterous individual or a rough expres-sion was heard upon the track to shock the nerves of the most sen-sitive lady; and no gaming was allowed of any kind; if there were any of the plug-uglies present, they were on their good behavior. A wonderful occasion indeed—not an intoxicated individual to be seen; not a pocket picked; not even a respectable citizen knocked down. Whoever heard of such a racetrack scene in this country be-fore? The unanimous voice among the knowing ones is that John Morrissey deserves the honor, and in the face of such overwhelm-ing testimony I cannot doubt the fact. Vive Morrissey.[38]

The trotting races only heightened anticipation for the Thoroughbreds. On opening day, a reporter for the *Times* ob-served: "Saratoga today is as full of transient visitors as a hive is of bees just before swarming time." That morning, race-goers "began making their way from downtown toward the track by 9 a.m. Thousands walked, and thousands more rode; omnibus-es, stagecoaches, carryalls, ambulances and wagons were run-ning to and fro. The grand stand was full to overflowing with fashionably dressed ladies and children, and well-behaved and well-dressed men. So orderly an assemblage, I believe, never was seen before on any other track in this country."[39] Morrissey de-served much credit for the orderliness of assemblage; he famous-ly insisted that patrons behave respectably, and when an unruly patron that week repeatedly ignored calls to be seated during a race, Morrissey "shook him as a big dog might a little puppy [un-til] the obnoxious individual agreed to obey orders rather than be ejected from the stand."[40]

One of the most accomplished runners in the history of American Thoroughbred racing, Kentucky won twenty consecutive races and twenty-one of twenty-three career starts, including the inaugural Travers Stakes, from 1863 to 1867. Oil on canvas, 1866, by Edward Troye (1808–1874).

Following an opening day highlighted by an impressive performance by a filly named Maiden, who took the Travers Stakes beneath her jockey Sewell, the second day of the meet included the inaugural running of the Saratoga Cup, which for years would be Saratoga's most prestigious event for older horses. With Gilpatrick aboard, John Hunter's bay colt Kentucky, who had won the previous year's Travers Stakes as a three-year-old, took the first Saratoga Cup, in front of ten thousand spectators. "As the races progress the crowd of visitors increases rather than diminishes," the *New York Times* reported midweek. "That so many people can find a place to eat or sleep in a town of so limited capacity as Saratoga [stretches credulity], and yet they do manage to live, or rather to exist, and all appear in comfortable condition. True there are many who sit up all night, indulging in a variety of nocturnal amusements, and take a little sleep during the day, but this class of visitors is comparatively small."[41]

The positive momentum for the Saratoga Association continued into the following year. "Pure air, fresh breezes, crisp fried potatoes, a great deal of very weak human nature, some exceedingly disagreeable water, and the New York morning papers are here," the *Times* reported at the height of the 1866 Saratoga social season. Only days before the start of the race meet, a fire had destroyed a major hotel in downtown Saratoga for the second consecutive summer, but that did not deter the racing enthusiasts. "The truth is," the *Times* continued, "that the majority of those who patronize the racing this year have come specially for that purpose, and not as visitors to the Springs; the number of prominent turfmen from the Southern and Western states [is] greater than was ever before assembled at one meeting."[42] After a solid opening day, which saw jockey Abe Hawkins, a former slave, take the Travers Stakes aboard Merrill, the crowds increased for the Saratoga Cup the following day.

"Large as had been the attendance on the first day, that on the second far surpassed it, both in brilliancy and numbers," the *Times* declared. "The spacious grand stand presented a beautiful appearance, filled as it was with ladies whose elegant and tasteful [fashion] gave additional attraction to the splendid scene. Order and decorum prevailed everywhere, and if the same admirable management which distinguish the direction of the Saratoga meeting is adopted at other places, racing will assuredly attain a height of popularity and patronage which it never before enjoyed in America."[43] For the second consecutive year, Kentucky won the Saratoga Cup, securing his place on any list of top runners of the era.

Morrissey's reputation, which had kept him from being listed among the Saratoga Association's executives, was ultimately of great value to the development of racing at Saratoga. His fame and notoriety gave the track instant publicity but also helped him to maintain order among the track patrons. Journalists reported that the track was safe and "respectable," which helped to convince some skeptics that racing at Saratoga was a suitable form of entertainment. Thus the Saratoga racecourse was neither a den of degenerates nor an exclusive enclave for the elite. From its very beginning, the racetrack at Saratoga, like the town itself, attracted a relatively wide spectrum of society. That broad appeal created early momentum for racing at Saratoga and provided a model for the commercialization of American sports more generally. Morrissey would continue to profit from the development of Saratoga as a center of commercialized sport, but in the meantime he would ride his reputation into a new realm—national politics.

5

Congressman

In addition to heralding a post–Civil War renaissance for Thoroughbred racing in America, the success of the early race meets at Saratoga was a testament to John Morrissey's talents as an organizer of commercialized sport and to the deftness with which he dealt with people from a variety of backgrounds. On the heels of his promising start as a racetrack operator, the possibility of a run for Congress soon began to be bandied about New York political circles. The notion that a boxer, a gangster, or a gambler could make a viable candidate for national elected office—let alone someone who had been involved in boxing, gangs, *and* gambling—would have once seemed preposterous. But predictions of Morrissey's political promise soon proved to be prescient, and in the fall of 1866 he was nominated as a candidate for the United States House of Representatives from the Fifth District in New York City by Tammany Hall Democrats, who by that time were heavily influenced by the notorious William M. "Boss" Tweed.[1]

Despite some complaints that Morrissey did not actually reside in the district and that he had reportedly donated a substantial amount of money to the local Democratic Party before his nomination, Morrissey accepted the candidacy at a convention that included representatives from the major local Democratic groups. "It is gratifying to me to receive these manifestations of the confidence of the different organizations that are represented here tonight," Morrissey said. "I stand here, gentlemen, as one of the humble exponents of the principles of the Democratic Party. That it is necessary for men in high position to fill our offices of honor, I do not believe; other men, who have heart, and have the disposition to place themselves before the great tribunal of a public vote, have the right, and I am one of those men. With all due respect for my opponents, I do not think that my Democratic friends will regret the action they have taken. They will always find me a trusty friend."[2]

In the immediate aftermath of the Civil War, which had concluded less than nineteen months earlier, American politics were rife with tension and dominated by the question of what to do with the conquered South. Republicans (called Radicals by their opponents) favored a policy of vengeance and actively pursued equal rights for recently freed blacks, while Democrats largely advocated for a return to "business as usual." Editorial commentators from both ends of the political spectrum used Morrissey's candidacy as an opportunity to air grievances, making the former boxer a lightning rod for political controversy. Critics of Morrissey felt that his background and "immoral" lifestyle should have disqualified him from holding a prestigious political office; one newspaper called him a "disgrace to the human species," asserting that "public decency and the dignity of the National Legislature have seldom been so boldly outraged."[3] Other editorialists were less harsh, opting for bad jokes at Morrissey's expense along the lines of the *Vinton (Ohio) Record*'s cheeky prediction that Morrissey would make a "bully" congressman.[4]

Journalists were critical not only of Morrissey but also of the Democrats who nominated him. The *Newark Daily Advertiser* reported:

John Morrissey, the noted prizefighter and gambler, has received the endorsement of Tammany Hall as the Democratic candidate for Congress in the Fifth District of New York. In this act Tammany and the Democracy have touched the lowest depths of degradation. In all the crime and wickedness of New York, in all that is demoralizing and vile, John Morrissey is the acknowledged chief. If he is elected—and there seems to be very little doubt of that—we have only to say that he is good enough for the party. They know him. There is no secrecy in his life, and when they send him to Congress they place themselves on his level and are no more entitled to the respect of decent men than is John Morrissey himself. Yet there are thousands of Democrats who are ready to vote for him. What a candidate! And what supporters![5]

Even Southern Democratic newspapers were critical. The *Louisville Courier* asked rhetorically, "What can the Northern Democrats expect but defeat when they are so careless of public opinion as to put forward as their candidates for high offices notorious blacklegs and prize-ring bruisers?"[6] Other newspapers defended Morrissey by pointing out the hypocrisy of a nation that damned him for having been a boxer while celebrating military heroes. "What right have these fellows to carp at John Morrissey, and condemn the [prize ring] as degrading and brutalizing in its tendencies and developments?" asked the *Urbana Union*. "What was the war between the North and South, but a combat between bullies of gigantic muscle? And what were battlefields but an immensely exaggerated prize ring?"[7]

Morrissey's extensive arrest record, which dated back to his teenage years, became a popular topic of discussion in newspapers across the nation. It was already well known that Morrissey had something of a criminal past, but the appearance of the details in print gave rise to a new round of moralistic condescension in the pages of the nation's dailies as election day neared. To provide his own explanation of his past, Morrissey (presumably with the help of an aide) drafted a widely published letter:

It is a duty not only to myself but to the people of the 5th Congressional District for whose support I am a candidate, that I should state the facts. When I was a boy, but 16 years of age, I and a few friends were engaged in an altercation with a party of young men, and in that altercation there was a door of a house kicked open. It was charged that I was one of those who kicked open the door and struck one of the opposing party. An affidavit was made by one of the men engaged in the quarrel that I had broken open the door and struck him. I was indicted for burglary and assault and battery. The indictment for burglary was never tried. The District Attorney regarded the charge as too frivolous to be prosecuted, and summarily dismissed it. I was tried for the assault and battery and found guilty.

Before entering upon my canvass for the position to which I aspire, I referred to my past life, which, until within the last eight years, was one of adventure, in consequence of the poverty of my parents and the few advantages I had in my early youth. I commenced to labor for my own livelihood and to assist in the support of my father and mother at the early age of ten years. At that time most boys are under the influence of domestic discipline, and have the advantage of regular educational training. Is it, therefore, strange that I should have committed errors in my early life? There are few boys that have not been guilty of a trifling assault and battery. If I had had influential parents and friends, I would have been permitted, probably, to have escaped with a reprimand; but having no one to say one kind word for me—a poor, rough boy, working in a foundry—I suffered the slight penalty due to my boyish folly.

During my whole life no man can say that I have ever wronged him, defrauded him of a dollar, or even broken my given word. I have had during the last eight years business relations and connections with many of the best men of this city, and not one of them will say I am other than a man of my word and of strict integrity; I have endeavored by my conduct to atone for the mistakes of my youth. Although successful in accumulating a competence, I have never forgotten that I was once poor. I have never turned a poor man from my door, or deserted a friend in his need. There has been much criticism in the newspapers in reference to my being a candidate for Congress. It is natural that I should be met with great opposition. A man who has passed through such varied and strange scenes of life as I have must expect to make bitter enemies and warm friends, and jealousies and hostilities are inseparable from political contests. But, Mr. Editor, I will state to you my motives in being a candidate for Congress.

I have one boy, who is now 12 years of age, who will have the benefit of the best education this country can afford, and will have better opportunities than I had, at his age, to start upon an honorable career. I feel it a duty that I owe to him, my only child, to make my record as clear and honorable as possible, that my manhood may atone for the follies and errors of my youth, and leave behind me memories of which my son in after years may be proud, and that will cast no shadow upon his path through life.[8]

Morrissey's letter only fueled the fires of public debate over the propriety of a gambling boxer's candidacy for Congress. "John seemed to think that if he could once write 'M.C.' [member of Congress] after his name, all the memory of the faro bank and of the prize-fighter's ring would fade away from men's minds, and his boy would grow up in delightful unconsciousness of his father's true character," the *Philadelphia Evening Telegraph* moaned. "We fear he has taken just the step to perpetuate all these memories, and to make them tenfold more vivid."[9]

The *New York Times* was similarly skeptical of Morrissey's justification of his candidacy:

Personally, we think much better of Morrissey than of some others who are candidates for Congress; we would take his word sooner, and trust him quicker with the care of any personal interest. But for all that, we do not think that the class to which he belongs, professionally and personally, [is] precisely the one from which our representatives in Congress should be selected. We can very well overlook his having kicked in a door in a frolic when he was sixteen years old, and might not perhaps deem it a fatal objection that he had badly battered Yankee Sullivan some years later in a prize fight. Nor do we deem it important any more than Morrissey himself does that we should confine our selection of representatives to the "aristocratic circles" of society. But it does not seem to us that we help the matter much, or place power strictly in the hands of working-men, by elevating professional gamblers to make our laws.[10]

Not surprisingly, New York's Tammany-influenced Fifth District elected Morrissey over a pair of opponents, a Republican named Eneas Elliott and the incumbent independent Democrat, General Nelson Taylor, by a substantial majority. "About half of the Republicans voted for Taylor, hoping thereby to defeat Morrissey," one newspaper explained, "but the Copperhead shoulder-hitters, blood-tubs, thieves, burglars, gamblers and ruffians constitute a clear majority of the votes of the Fifth District of New York City."[11]

An Ohio newspaper howled, "His election is, to say the least, a burning shame, and a blot upon the page of American History. Won't it be fun, though, to see the little boot-blacks 'skedaddle' when he approaches them, and hear them whispering to one another, 'Da's de man what *kills* folks wid his fists!' while the elite of the city will instinctively clutch their pocketbooks as they pass him, as if in fear that he may try to regain a portion of the $180,000 spent to secure his election."[12] A religious magazine lamented that Morrissey's election was "a deep and burning disgrace to the American people. A party once ruled by Jefferson and Madison, now by Morrissey!"[13]

Soon after the election results were reported, newspapers began using the title "the Honorable" when referring to Morrissey

Morrissey achieved some modicum of respectability for himself and his family as a congressman, but he never lost his connection to gambling and prizefighting, as this cartoon, originally published in the *New York Daily Graphic,* c. 1875, illustrates. (University of Wisconsin–Madison Archives)

by name in print. For example, the *Ashtabula Weekly Telegraph* reported, "Plain John Morrissey, the Bruiser whose police record covers nine indictments for assault and battery, with and without intention to kill, and two indictments and one conviction for burglary, has by the choice of the electors of the 5th congressional district of New York, become 'Honorable' John Morrissey."[14] Eventually newspapers dropped the quotation marks when referring to Morrissey as "Honorable," but the irony of using that adjective to describe a former boxer and gambler remained.

Marcus "Brick" Pomeroy, a divisive conservative Democratic commentator cantankerously came to Morrissey's defense in his widely read editorial column:

The Radical papers are making a great ado over [Morrissey's] election by a majority of thousands. Let us see a little. Who and what is Morrissey? He is liberal to the poor, giving thousands of dollars yearly to objects of charity; he pays a hundred cents on the dollar for all he owes; he moves in the best society of New York; he is a clear-headed business man, with broad, liberal, national views.

He was a poor man—so was Abe Lincoln. Morrissey was a mechanic—Lincoln was a rail-splitter. Morrissey talks, acts, [and] appears like a gentleman of sense. Lincoln told smutty stories, stitched hogs' eyelids together to blind them so he could drive them—poked his knuckles into peoples' ribs, and guffawed at his own smartness.

He is not of those chicken-stealing, Christ-forgetting, wench-loving, nigger-worshipping, Bible-bangers, such as turn their sacred desks into political stands and wallow in the worldly pool of politics.

And if we were on a dying bed, in need of heavenly intercession, we would give more for the prayers of muscular, liberal, gentlemanly John Morrissey than for those of the majority of orthodox so-called Christians of the present age.[15]

The notion that the man who had risen to national fame as a boxer, gangland operator, and gambler was the same man who was now congressman-elect was difficult for many to come to terms with, as evidenced by the reaction a journalist from Cincinnati had upon encountering Morrissey in person, for the first time in a decade, in a New York hotel. "In the Democratic Congressman of today I tried to recognize the pugilist of ten years since," the reporter said, "but I couldn't—nor could I detect even the poker player of yesterday."[16] As depicted by journalists, Morrissey's two-sided public persona—alternately a monster and an embodiment of the American dream—fueled the public's craving for any information about what seemed to be a fascinating character. Even before his election, Morrissey had been sufficiently famous for newspapers to report on an injury to his son. "A son of John Morrissey, of pugilistic fame, while watching the antics of a monkey yesterday afternoon, ventured too near the animal, and had two of his fingers bitten," the *New York Evening Post* explained, weeks before Morrissey's election. "Today Mrs. Morrissey found the organ-grinder who kept the offending monkey, and had him taken to Police Headquarters. After telling the facts to Inspector Carpenter, she was surprised to learn that the official had no power to imprison the organ grinder or to kill the monkey. She was advised to go to Jefferson Market and enter a complaint before the presiding magistrate; she was unwilling to do this, but declared she would kill the monkey herself."[17]

Once his status as a congressman was added to his "pugilistic fame," Morrissey's celebrity was only heightened, and the press reported any details that it could find about him and his family. Many articles focused on his wife's wardrobe, her jewelry, and other conspicuous displays of the family's purported wealth. Not long after the election, a Philadelphia newspaper published a report from a wedding in Troy, New York, attended by Mrs. Morrissey: "The lady was certainly attired far in advance of any of her sex who were present, and it has been said that the value of the precious stones which adorned her person would purchase not only all the dresses worn in the church, but the edifice and its entire furniture."[18]

The press even found Susie Morrissey's means of transportation to be noteworthy. "Mrs. John Morrissey drives in a coach richly trimmed with gold, silver and silk, and valued at $2,000," said the *Troy Times*. "The horses are presents to Mrs. Morrissey from Commodore Vanderbilt and another New York gentleman, and carry harness costing $1,000. Young Morrissey rides a stallion not much larger than a Shetland pony that can make his mile in 2:40. The turn-out, as a whole, might do for royalty itself."[19]

But semi-sneering journalistic allusions to the Morrisseys' material wealth were countered by reports of their generosity. "Say what you will of the Hon. John Morrissey (and we will say nothing) we know that Mrs. John Morrissey has many admirable qualities," the *New York Home Journal* asserted. "It is a universal fact that she is wealthy, but unlike many wealthy people, she is very charitable and liberal almost to a fault. Few go to her in need and depart empty handed. By the shop girls, [on] Broadway, at the establishments where Mrs. Morrissey deals, she is much liked, nay adored, for she is constantly making them presents or doing some act of great kindness for them."[20] Another newspaper reported, "Mrs. John Morrissey did a kind thing to a poor crippled boy in the cars between Troy and New York last week. She found him a comfortable seat, pillowed his head on her rich shawl, bought oranges for him, paid his fare and watched over the lad while he enjoyed a refreshing slumber."[21] Newspapers also regularly credited John Morrissey for rising above his humble origins and for providing for his recently located destitute sister and supporting a handful of war veterans and impoverished children.[22]

Few men had ever entered Congress under the scrutiny Morrissey faced as he came to Washington in March 1867 for the start of his first term. Some actually had high hopes for what

Morrissey could accomplish, given the attention that surrounded him. The *New York Times* acknowledged the potential impact Morrissey could have in Washington and called on him to stake a moderate position between the Radical Republicans and the Copperhead Democrats.[23]

He would prove to be far more of a Copperhead than a Radical, but Morrissey did occasionally stray from the Democratic Party line. One example was his vote to award a pension to Mary Todd Lincoln, which was in keeping with his lifelong tendency toward compassion for women and children and gave some credence to a line attributed to him: "[I] don't care which party wins provided the thing comes out right."[24] As he later told an interviewer, "While I am a staunch Democrat, I am so unquestionably [financially] sound that I could afford to vote in opposition to my party whenever I thought that mere partisanship diverted it from paths of duty and right and patriotism."[25]

But anyone hoping that Morrissey would become an active participant on the House floor was ultimately disappointed, as Morrissey was conspicuously silent in his time in Congress. One newspaper joked that during his first visit to the House of Representatives, Morrissey pointed toward the Speaker's desk and asked whether that was "where the referee sat."[26] While that "news item" was obviously an attempt at humor, it betrayed the modest expectations that most Americans had for New York's Fifth District representative. Morrissey's appointment to the Revolutionary Pensions Committee reflected those expectations, and the *New York Sun* published a purported account of how Morrissey received that particular appointment:

Mr. [Schuyler] Colfax, who was then Speaker, was busily making up the Committees, and happened to be conversing with three or four members. He observed Morrissey repeatedly crossing by the door, as though desirous of entering. At last, after the departure of Mr. Colfax's visitors, Morrissey stealthily crept up to the door, took a peep, saw that no one was there, and entered. Approaching Mr. Colfax, he said: "Mr. Speaker, I have a fine box of Havana cigars I am going to send you. Will you accept them?"

"Oh yes, certainly," replied Mr. Colfax. "Anything in that line is acceptable."

"All right," said Morrissey. After a pause, he suddenly broke out: "Mr. Speaker, I have a favor to ask. I want you to put me on a certain committee."

"Leave the cigars [aside], and tell me what one it is," replied Mr. Colfax.

Morrissey made a strenuous effort, closed his fist, and as he brought it down on the desk, said: "I want you to put me on that Committee where I will have damn little work to do."

"All right," said Mr. Colfax. When the Committees were announced, the name of the Hon. John Morrissey was found bringing up the rear on the Committee on Revolutionary Pensions.[27]

Regardless of the literal accuracy of the story, Morrissey's spot on a committee whose purpose was to address pensions from a war nearly a century old placed him far from the center of congressional power. Nevertheless, when the Congress convened for the swearing-in ceremony, Morrissey attracted keen interest from curious spectators and journalists. "When he made his appearance to be sworn in, the anxiety of the House and the galleries to get a glimpse of him was intense," the *Times* reported. "Members crowded around his seat to congratulate him, and the brilliant array of ladies who on this occasion were scattered all over the House, gave evidence of something more than curiosity concerning him." Seated near the front of the chamber, Morrissey was "genteelly dressed, perspired quite freely, and was kept busy mopping his face with a large white pocket handkerchief." After being sworn in, his first public act was to join his fellow Democrats in entering a protest against the exclusion of southern representatives from their seats in Congress.[28]

Perhaps because caricaturists often depicted him as a violent brute, many Washingtonians were surprised, upon seeing Morrissey in person for the first time, by the dignity with which the former boxing champion carried himself.

Through his first week in the legislature Morrissey continued to be a source of public fascination and received a nearly constant barrage of autograph requests from congressional pages. Journalists who had never actually seen Morrissey in person were surprised to learn that he dressed more in the manner of a sophisticate than a gangster: "Morrissey is garbed with unexceptional care to the properties of his position," one reporter noted.

"Always in broadcloth and finest linen, he comports himself both to and from the representative chamber like a dignified and trustful guardian of the public weal."[29]

For the remainder of his first year in Congress, Morrissey retained his celebrity status in Washington but managed to avoid any real political activity. Early in 1868 he voted against a supplement to the previous year's Reconstruction Act before heading off to Hot Springs, Arkansas, to be treated for, according to various reports, asthma, rheumatism, or a kidney ailment, returning east in time for the summer recess. He missed the congressional vote to impeach President Andrew Johnson on charges of violation of the Tenure of Office Act, but Morrissey would almost certainly have voted against impeachment. Along with much of the powerful New York Democratic congressional delegation, Morrissey had a good relationship with the president; he regularly met with him regarding federal appointments for New York positions (including one for his friend and future U.S. president Chester A. Arthur as surveyor of the Port of New York). During the Democratic convention later that summer, Morrissey wrote Johnson a note urging the president to "be deaf to false counsels, and when you have done your duty the civilization of the age will solve the balance of the problem." Morrissey was even mentioned in murky and unsubstantiated rumors to have been involved in a bribery plot regarding the deciding vote in Johnson's acquittal before the Senate in May.[30]

As the 1868 fall elections approached, the press paid more attention to Morrissey's handling of bets on the presidential race than to his own chances at reelection (gambling on election results was quite popular at the time). But the *New York Sun* did give him a vote of confidence, stating, "Mr. Morrissey is a fitting and worthy representative of the Fifth District. He has served in Congress with respectability. He has gained reputation by his service, both as a man of honor and a man of sense. His votes were all in accordance with the policy of his party. Why, then, should he not be re-nominated by the Democracy of the Fifth District? If he is, he will be re-elected of course."[31]

The ever-churning factionalism of New York City politics made his nomination less than certain, but he was ultimately nominated and won the election comfortably. The unsuccessful Republican candidate filed a lawsuit contesting the results of the election on the basis that "Mr. Morrissey has not had a legal residence in this country of sufficient length of time to entitle him to a seat in Congress." But that Republican had no more success in his effort than did those who questioned the citizenship of President Barack Obama a century and a half later.[32]

That winter Morrissey was regularly absent from Washington. In March a southern newspaper noted that Morrissey had appeared at his desk on the House floor for the first time since December: "Of this we do not complain, as, except in so far as his negligence indicates a perfect willingness to receive the public money without a shadow of return, we think his absence from the Halls of National Legislation was a thing to be thankful for."[33] But later that week he did manage to attend President Ulysses S. Grant's inaugural ball, where the press reported that Mrs. Morrissey "was resplendent in black velvet, point lace and diamonds."[34]

That fall Morrissey's name appeared in newspapers as one of the many victims of an attempt to corner the gold market by financiers James Fisk and Jay Gould. Morrissey lost a reported $80,000 (sixteen times his annual congressional salary) as a result of the plot when the gold markets crashed on "Black Friday," and he blamed Fisk. "Thousands of men have been permanently ruined by a band of thieves, guilty of the worst thieving that has ever happened in any country in the world," Morrissey hissed.[35] Though reports of Morrissey personally threatening Fisk with bodily harm were exaggerated, Morrissey was one of a select few who managed to get his money returned to him. The *New York Times* explained, "The summary process used was not of a corporeal nature, but simply an intimation, in very emphatic terms, through a mutual acquaintance, of what would follow in a week, or in six weeks, or whenever [Fisk] dared show himself outside his entrenched office if the money was not forthcoming at once to the uttermost penny. The money came."[36]

As he continued to find other matters to occupy his time and attention, Morrissey's attendance record in Congress further deteriorated. According to one report, between early December 1869 and mid-July 1870, Morrissey was absent 120 out of the 166 days Congress was scheduled to be in session.[37] For much of the winter, he was tending to a "dangerous illness of his wife," but his presence was irregular even in the spring, after she had recovered from her unspecified ailment.[38] Morrissey "has been absent from his seat for months together," the *Times* reported. "When he suddenly reappeared on Monday, people stared at him as if he had descended—or ascended—from another world. He has been away from his post nearly four months."[39]

In fact, Morrissey had spent much of the early spring in New York, neck deep in a local political battle. Morrissey had begun to fall out of favor with Boss Tweed and his cronies as early as 1868, in part over a disagreement regarding a local election for sheriff. By 1870 Morrissey was one of the leaders of the Young Democracy, a New York City political movement, organized at his Twenty-Fourth Street gambling house, whose members, calling themselves "reformers," hoped to seize control of Tammany Hall and the Democratic Party from Tweed and his political gang. Some of the Young Democracy members wanted a bigger cut of the Tweed Ring's graft, some were disappointed at unfulfilled political ambition, and some simply disliked Tweed or other members of his circle.[40]

Despite their ambition, the Young Democracy members' push for power was short-lived, as the group was soundly drubbed at the Tammany Society's April election of officers. The trouncing, dubbed a "Waterloo defeat" by the press, sealed Morrissey's fate with Boss Tweed, who effectively excommunicated Morrissey from the party, eliminating any realistic chance for a third term in Congress.[41] But given his dismal attendance record in Washington, and the other sporting and business interests on his plate, Morrissey was likely not personally devastated by the chance to spend his time and energy elsewhere.[42]

In late December Morrissey was in Jem Mace's saloon on Twenty-Third Street in Manhattan, drunk, and drew his derringer. According to one version of the story, a "desperate character" had provoked Morrissey by spitting in his face. Another version identified Morrissey as the unprovoked instigator. However the altercation may have begun, the situation was diffused when the proprietor of the establishment, himself a former English boxing champion, hustled Morrissey to a back room and locked him inside. Given that his congressional tenure was at an end, published reports of the incident did not cause the uproar that they might have had he been heading back to Washington for a third congressional term. In the circles to which he would soon be returning, there was nothing terribly unusual about a round of late-night fisticuffs at a local tavern, even if it did involve the "Honorable" John Morrissey.[43]

6

Impresario

When his second, and final, congressional term came to an end in March 1871, Morrissey was happy to be free of his legislative responsibilities. As he made his way down to New Orleans for the race meet at the Metairie Racetrack that spring, he told a reporter that his time in Congress had cost him "not less than half a million" in foregone gambling opportunities.[1] While in New Orleans, Morrissey made up for lost time by purchasing a horse named Defender and placing a bet against him in the horse's next race that yielded a $30,000 profit. At the conclusion of the Metairie meet, Morrissey headed to Saratoga, where another record-breaking tourist season was expected.[2]

Saratoga had hosted more than one hundred thousand visitors the previous year, and many of them had spent time in Morrissey's lavish new casino called the Club House, a stately Italianate mansion adjacent to the Congress Springs Park. Called "a gorgeous, gilded, glittering, trap-door to perdition" by one clergyman, the casino was the finest in America and "furnished like a palace." Guests were met by an elegantly dressed doorman, and Morrissey, still quite physically imposing despite having left the prize ring more than a decade earlier, added an air of decorum as he quietly presided over the activity in the gaming parlors and dining hall, where extravagant dinners were served nightly to the patrons.[3]

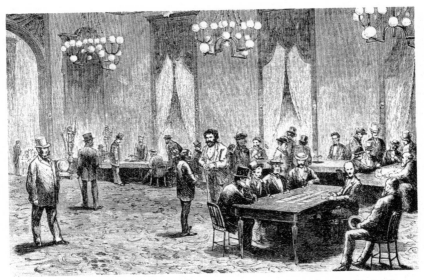

When it was opened for the 1870 tourist season, Morrissey's Club House was the finest in North America and rivaled any in the world. (Courtesy of New York Historical Society, New York City)

An expansion of the facility, including new parlors for heavy bettors as well as additional dining space, was ready for the 1871 season. When the improved casino was opened for business, it was "more gorgeously fitted up, decorated, and furnished than any other place in Europe," one reviewer raved.[4] In the new configuration there was also a well-appointed room devoted to betting on horse racing and other sports, where club members could read newspapers from across the country and receive stock quotes from Wall Street via telegraph.[5]

Local religious groups waged a public-relations battle against the Club House in hopes of forcing its closure, but Morrissey had ingratiated himself with Saratoga business and political leaders, who clearly saw the casino's upside. "Saratoga is fast assuming the position of the Baden-Baden of America, and Morrissey is its architect," the *Memphis Public Ledger* declared, echoing Morrissey's local defenders. "His club-house is one of the most elegant buildings of its kind in the land. For beauty

Following Morrissey's death, the facility would pass to Morrissey's partners, Albert Spencer and Charles Reed. It would eventually be acquired by Richard Canfield, who enhanced the building and grounds and presided over a new golden era at the casino until he sold the facility to the city in the wake of antigambling reform measures. It was given National Historic Landmark status in 1987 and is now home to the Saratoga Springs History Museum. Postcard c. 1970s.

and sumptuousness of its table it has no equal, it is said, in Europe. The track is one of the best in America. This, with nearly all the modern improvements of Saratoga, [is] Morrissey's handiwork."[6] The article went on to claim that John Morrissey was a millionaire. Journalists had made wild guesses as to the extent of Morrissey's personal wealth for years, and usually it was greatly overestimated. But, given the nature of his major sources of income—gambling and stock speculation—any measurement of Morrissey's fortune was necessarily subject to volatile change. Some speculated that Morrissey's casino in Saratoga raked in half a million dollars annually, and the widespread belief that he was fabulously wealthy only enhanced his influence in sporting and political circles on the local and national levels.

Although women were not allowed to gamble in his casino, Morrissey welcomed them to have a look around in the late morning and early afternoon. One morning, according to a story in the *New York Sun,* a particularly devout lady was shown around the building. As she reached the exit following her tour, she turned to a casino employee and solemnly addressed him. "Sir, you are Mr. Morrissey, I presume?" she said.

"No, madam, my name is Lewis—I am one of the attachés of the establishment," the man replied.

"Well, then, sir," continued the lady, with her right hand pointing to the ceiling, "I would like to ask you one question. What good will it do you to gain all the money in the world in this house, and then lose your soul?"

"We don't play for souls, madam," replied Lewis. "We only play for money."[7]

Skeptical citizens often joined the morning tours, including some clergymen. At least one minister was won over by his visit, remarking that the Club House was "too beautiful to be so bad." A Presbyterian minister from Brooklyn named Theodore L. Culyer disagreed, writing in the *New York Evangelist*, "In plain English, *that house is a hell,* and in eternity the curses of its inmates will be visited on the head of him who opened it as a road to ruin."[8] When whispers began to circulate suggesting that women were being allowed into the casino, Morrissey quickly published a letter that would be reprinted in various New York newspapers to reassure readers. "The report is going the rounds of the newspapers that my house is open to ladies to gamble in," Morrissey wrote. "I desire to contradict the story flatly through your columns. I have lived in Saratoga nine years and no lady has ever gambled, nor will ever gamble, in my house. By request, ladies have been admitted to look at the house and furniture, but the comment it has occasioned, far and near, prompts me to decline any further visits from them. Furthermore, my house is intended for visitors, not residents of Saratoga."[9]

Even if Morrissey could no longer allow them in his gaming

house, ladies were still an important part of the clientele at the racetrack. Because of the track's early success and the business it generated for the town, all but the most strident reformers were content to leave Morrissey and his casino alone. Morrissey "has made the track one of the great racing places of America," the *New York Times* explained, "and so far has undoubtedly done much for Saratoga. Therefore the clubhouse exists on sufferance."[10] Part of the appeal of the Saratoga track was the relative scarcity of "improper characters" there, which was a source of pride for Morrissey. On the first day of racing at the 1870 meet, Morrissey saw a gang of "five notorious thieves and desperadoes from New York" approaching the track's front entrance in a carriage. When the leader of the group, who had shot a man in Albany a few months earlier, attempted to purchase tickets, Morrissey asked the man whether he was certain that he wanted to enter. "You might think better of it," Morrissey added.

The man fingered a pistol and said, "This is a public track and I'm going in."

"I'll make you think it is a church before I am through with you, and if you dare draw that pistol on me, I'll make you eat it," Morrissey replied. Police eventually detained the man, and Morrissey earned plaudits in the press for his continued vigilance.[11]

As the 1871 tourist season hit full stride, the most anticipated event on the American racing calendar was the Saratoga Cup. Although the race would be contested by only two horses, they were the two top four-year-olds in the country, Longfellow and Kingfisher. Despite a less-than-regal-looking head (he had what horsemen called a "Roman nose"), Longfellow was one of the greatest runners of his era. His owner, "Uncle" John Harper, claimed that he had named the horse not for the famous poet but because his colt had the longest legs "of any feller I ever seen."[12] New Yorkers, and particularly journalists, got a kick out of Harper, a Kentucky horseman who was more backwoodsman than stereotypical Kentucky aristocrat. Uncle John had received little formal education, but he was not the rube he was often made out to be. He had found success in the racehorse business, and Longfellow was the finest animal he ever bred or owned. Harper was also Longfellow's nominal trainer, though his African American stable workers—some of them former slaves—appeared to all observers to do the great majority of the work with the horse.[13]

Longfellow's opponent in the Saratoga Cup, Kingfisher, had recently been purchased by August Belmont, a New York financier and Democratic Party power broker, who had been born in what is now Germany. Belmont was sent to America as a young man by his employers, the Rothschild international banking consortium, to tend to some business affairs, and he remained there for the rest of his life. He changed his name from Schonberg and converted from Judaism to his fiancée's Episcopalian faith before they married (she was the daughter of Commodore Matthew Perry, who was credited with opening Japan to trade with the West in the 1850s). Although Kingfisher had won the Travers Stakes in 1870 and was widely considered to be the top horse on the East Coast, Longfellow was the solid favorite, on the strength of his recent performance in the Monmouth Cup and his impressive morning workouts.

Rain showers earlier in the day had subsided as the two-horse field made its way onto the track for the Saratoga Cup. When Longfellow came into view of the grandstand, a swarm of spectators rushed onto the track to get a closer look. Morrissey and several track constables had to clear the crowd out of the way so that the horses could proceed to the starting line. Charles Wheatley was the starter for the race, and, as he later recalled, after Kingfisher broke quickly Longfellow "wheeled and gathered himself for a spring. He seemed to rise to an awful height, then he sprang forward, and in a twinkling he was in the front." According to another observer, Longfellow "seemed to float upon the air. A more perfect gait was never witnessed on the turf. He seemed to make no exertion whatsoever, and as the two passed the Judges' stand in the three-quarter stretch the spectators rose in a body, regardless of the cries of the police—Handkerchiefs begin to wave and cheers to break forth."[14] After a record first mile in 1:40, according to official timer H. P. McGrath, Longfellow extended his lead to six lengths. As they exited the final turn, Kingfisher's jockey asked his colt for more. He managed to close the sizable gap but could get no closer than three lengths to the long-striding Longfellow.[15]

"The excitement that ensued was unparalleled," the *Charleston Daily News* declared. "Men rushed about with tears in their eyes, vowing that such a horse as this was never foaled. The only perfectly cool person was Longfellow's owner, old John Harper, who tottered along leaning on his cane and shouting directions to the negro boys who were grooming the victor. Turfmen say they never witnessed a more beautiful or exciting contest."[16] The attention that major racing events at Saratoga were receiving in the national press confirmed that by working to realize his vision of top-class racing at Saratoga, Morrissey was influencing not only the sport of horse racing but also the identity of an entire region, making Saratoga a magnet for the growing number of American sports enthusiasts.

The fastest-growing sport in post–Civil War America was baseball, and, by virtue of his association with the Troy Haymakers baseball club, Morrissey would be implicated in one of the most famous scandals in the young history of a game that was notoriously corrupt in its early years.[17] From eclectic roots of stick and ball games from Continental Europe and Britain, baseball emerged as a popular diversion among upwardly mobile New York men who gathered to play in city parks and at New Jersey's Elysian Fields in the 1840s in sociable fraternal outings. In 1857 fourteen leading New York City clubs agreed to some standard rules, including nine players per team and nine innings per game. The following year the National Association of Baseball Players was formed in response to the mushrooming popularity of the sport in cities down the East Coast and across the Midwest. The amiable climate of early baseball had grown more competitive, and a market for top talent quickly emerged, despite the fact that paying players was technically forbidden by the rules of the association. Teams managed to circumvent these rules, however, and Boss Tweed was at the forefront of this "under the table" system as he could attract top players to his New York Mutuals by providing them with government jobs. In response to this troubling development, the association created a professional category at its December 1868 meeting.[18]

The Cincinnati Red Stockings were the first to field an all-professional team under the new rules. The 1867 Reds had been embarrassed by their 53–10 defeat at the hands of the Washington Nationals and decided to import talent the following year. That team was competitive but lost money, and Cincinnati leaders saw that they would need to bring in even better ballplayers, so they made the bold move of spending $10,000 on players' salaries for the 1869 season, going "all-in" on a professional experiment. The Reds won their first thirty-nine games that year, including a 4–2 victory over Boss Tweed's New York Mutuals in front of ten thousand spectators, including Morrissey, in what was described as one of the greatest games ever played. A week earlier, Cincinnati had narrowly defeated the Troy Haymakers 37–31, and Morrissey had learned all he needed from that game to profit from a bet on Cincinnati against the Mutuals.[19]

To some it appeared that the Reds were unbeatable, creating juicy betting opportunities for supporters of the Haymakers, including Morrissey, when that team came to Cincinnati in August. The Haymakers were one of early baseball's most successful organizations and, after the Mutuals, also one of the most notoriously corrupt.[20] The *Cincinnati Commercial* commented, "The Haymakers, while strong players, are not of good reputation [and] are used like loaded dice and marked cards." Morrissey had something of an ambiguous relationship with the Troy club.

Some have referred to him as an owner, but superfan or booster would be a better description. Rumors circulated the morning of the game that some of the Reds players had been approached by New York gamblers, including associates of Morrissey's, and those murmurings only grew louder when star Reds pitcher Asa Brainard gave up six runs in the first inning, four of which came with two outs, on three Cincinnati fielding errors. But the Red Stockings answered with ten runs in the second inning, six of which came after a controversial "safe" call by the umpire on a play at the plate that would have been the final out of the inning. In the fifth inning, after the umpire called a Troy base runner out at second, Haymakers president James McKeon stormed onto the field, pointing his cane in the umpire's direction, and threatened to remove his team if any other close plays were called against his team. Cincinnati captain Harry Wright offered to find a new umpire, hoping to deprive McKeon of any plausible excuse in the event of a Reds victory, but McKeon refused.[21]

With the score tied at seventeen in the following inning, Cincinnati right fielder Cal McVey tipped a foul ball that landed behind the plate. Troy's catcher, Bill Craven, swiped at the ball but caught it only after what were clearly multiple bounces. The catcher held the ball up dramatically, signaling that he believed he had caught the ball cleanly. The umpire said "no catch." As promised, the Haymakers president called the team off the field, and the players quickly began to pack their equipment and head for the omnibus that would take them to their hotel. The Reds president tried to dissuade the Haymakers from leaving, but the partisan crowd rushed onto the field, creating the potential for a riot. City police emerged to maintain order, and the Haymakers were allowed to quickly make their way from the field as the frustrated spectators lobbed bottles, rocks, and vegetables.[22]

The umpire assured the crowd that Cincinnati had won the game, but his decision was subject to official review by the association. Later that year, at the association's national convention, the judiciary committee decided that the game was a tie, prompting suspicion of undue influence by the Troy club. But the game remained a tie in the record books, the only blemish on an otherwise perfect season for the Cincinnati Red Stockings. Morrissey was widely reported to have had as much as $60,000 riding on the game, and though no specific evidence of chicanery emerged, in the minds of those who believed that the Reds had been wrongfully deprived of perfection, he was guilty of *something*. Fairly or not, the events that unfolded on the playing field provided fodder for conspiracy theorists and served as an indication that, while he had achieved much since his fighting days, the taint of Morrissey's past still lingered.[23]

The following year, American sports enthusiasts were riveted by the possibility that two of the best racehorses Americans had seen in years, Longfellow and Harry Bassett, might meet on the racetrack to determine supremacy. Harry Bassett, a handsome chestnut colt purchased for $315 as a yearling in Kentucky by Colonel David McDaniel, had completed an undefeated three-year-old season the year before, including victories in the Travers and Belmont Stakes, and was the top four-year-old in America. Bassett was trained by his owner, Colonel McDaniel, a native of Ireland who settled in Virginia, where he was a prominent horse trader and slave dealer, before establishing a Thoroughbred breeding operation in New Jersey called Stony Brook Stud. McDaniel was convinced that he had the greatest horse in America. The only serious rival that remained for Harry Bassett to vanquish was Uncle John Harper's Longfellow, now five years old, who had secured his status as the top older horse in the nation with his victory in the Saratoga Cup the previous year. McDaniel, once described as "not a scholar" and "a man of the greatest simplicity," challenged Harper and Longfellow to a match race, to which Harper responded that anyone who wanted to test his big brown horse could do so at the Monmouth Cup at Monmouth Park in New Jersey.[24]

Harry Bassett with jockey James Rowe and owner David McDaniel. The son of legendary stallion Lexington won fourteen consecutive races, including the 1871 Belmont and Travers Stakes. "Ready for the Signal," artist John Cameron (1828–1876), Currier & Ives, c. 1872. (Library of Congress)

As a sport and a business, horse racing was growing by leaps and bounds each year in the North, thanks in part to three former associates of John Morrissey's: Leonard Jerome, John Chamberlain, and H. P. McGrath. These men had been instrumental in founding two of the finest racecourses in America: Jerome Park, in what is now the Bronx, and Monmouth Park, near Long Branch, New Jersey. Those tracks followed Saratoga's model in a wave of late nineteenth-century racetrack construction in the North, which was enjoying a post–Civil War economic boom. Jerome had been one of the original members of the Saratoga Association, and Chamberlain had been a part owner, along with McGrath, of one of Morrissey's Manhattan casinos in the 1860s. In addition to McGrath, Chamberlain's partners in Monmouth Park included Tammany Hall's Boss Tweed, as well as robber barons James Fisk and Jay Gould.[25]

Set for July 2, 1872, the Monmouth Cup was shaping up to

be a race for the ages, and Harper adorned Longfellow's railroad car for the trip to New Jersey with a banner that read, "Longfellow on his way to Long Branch to meet his friend Harry Bassett." Race fans and gamblers came from New Jersey, Philadelphia, and various parts of the South and West, but the majority, twenty-five thousand or more, traveled from New York City, and the large crowd at Monmouth reflected the broadening popularity of American sports. "They were of all classes," the *Times* reported. "There was the rough, pure and simple, there was his brother with the tawdry trappings of Tammany, there was the sturdy laborer, there was the intelligent mechanic of whom we have heard so much during the present strikes. There were tradesmen, bankers, brokers, railway men, [and] oil men."[26]

Heavy betting abounded around the racecourse, much of it facilitated by the newfangled pari-mutuel machines recently installed at the track. Imported from France, the pari-mutuel system, which proved to be popular with people who could not afford the high stakes of auction pools, allowed patrons to bet as little as five dollars on the horse of their choice, with the final odds determined by the aggregate amount bet on each runner. Morrissey would implement the system at Saratoga later that summer, but at Monmouth, it was noted in the newspapers, he "invested" heavily in Harry Bassett, betting more than $25,000 with friends and bookmakers.[27]

The starting line for the two-and-a-half-mile race was positioned on the far side of the one-mile track, across from the grandstand, and a series of scratches had left Longfellow and Harry Bassett as the only starters. At the tap of the drum, the race began cleanly, and the two contestants were neck-and-neck as they passed the stands for the first time and rounded the track again. With a mile left to go, Longfellow took the lead, which seemed to increase with every stride down the backstretch. Harry Bassett's fifteen-year-old jockey, Jimmy Rowe, who would later become a legendary trainer, urged his mount forward, but

Bassett did not respond. When his tail flew up, the spectators knew he was beaten, and Longfellow cantered home to win by a hundred yards.[28]

The race—particularly its uncompetitive finish—failed to meet lofty expectations, but it had attracted a larger crowd than anyone could remember at a horse race.[29] The *Times* had called the Monmouth Cup the "great racing event of 1872," but that title would last only two weeks until the Saratoga Cup, which the newspaper dubbed "the Greatest Contest in American Turf History," provided Harry Bassett a chance at redemption.[30] Morrissey entered his horse Discovery in an attempt to add some additional gambling intrigue to the event, but he was almost entirely ignored by bettors and spectators, who knew that it was a two-horse race. The pool rooms and casinos were crowded until the early hours of the morning before the big race, with most of the money being placed on Longfellow.[31]

The day of the race, the streets were clogged with racing fans by mid-morning. The *Times* observed, "The grandstand was occupied much earlier than usual—every one hurrying from the breakfast table in order to secure a good seat from whence to witness the great race. Carriages followed one another in rapid succession, and pedestrians waded through the dust as though they cared nothing for it. All along the route one could catch scarce a sound save the words Bassett and Longfellow." The first race of the day was the Saratoga Stakes for two-year-olds. The list of owners with entries was a who's-who of leaders of the American turf, including August Belmont, Leonard Jerome, William R. Travers, and Kentuckian Daniel Swigert. But the race was won by a colt named Catesby, owned by Oden Bowie, a former governor of Maryland.[32]

When Longfellow and Harry Bassett made their way onto the track for the start of the two-and-a-quarter-mile Saratoga Cup, "a wild shout of delight was given by the spectators. Countless thousands of eyes were strained in that direction, and each individual almost heard his neighbor's heart beat, so still was the vast concourse of people. Lips were dry and eyes were moist from the momentary tension."[33] As the horses were being arranged at the starter's direction, a reporter observed the nervous crowd: "It was most painful to look around and study the varied expressions of countenance. Some looked as grave as judges, others were nervous and trembling; others again looked as though bordering on an attack of acute mania."[34]

At the starter's orders the horses broke quickly, and before the horses had reached the grandstand, Defender was out of the race, already five lengths behind the others. When Longfellow and Harry Bassett passed the spectators for the first time, with Bassett leading by half a length, Morrissey noticed something was wrong with Longfellow and cried out, "Longfellow's beat." As the horses passed the stand, "one uproarious shout rent the air, and every one hustled and jostled in spite of the earnest entreaties of the police that all would keep their seats."[35]

Bassett maintained his lead, but Longfellow never fell farther than a length behind, matching his rival stride for stride as they thundered around the course, pulling to within a head, then falling back half a length. With a half mile to the finish line, Harry Bassett's lead was three-quarters of a length, and Longfellow's supporters held their collective breath in anticipation of a late burst of speed, but it never came, and Bassett stretched his advantage to a full length as they crossed the finish line. The final time of 3:59 knocked two seconds off the course record set by Kentucky in the first Saratoga Cup.

"The scene which followed is indescribable," wrote one reporter, who then described the scene: "The colored jockeys and trainers yelled like maniacs, tumbled over one another, and fought to get to the judges' stand first. Hats and sticks literally darkened the air, and I am not sure that many a colored stable-boy was not tossed aloft for joy. In the grand stand men shouted

Harry Bassett and Longfellow, two of the most successful and popular race-horses of the late nineteenth century, met twice in the summer of 1872. Longfellow won the Monmouth Cup on July 2, but Harry Bassett had revenge in the Saratoga Cup two weeks later in what would be Longfellow's final race. "Harry Bassett and Longfellow in their great races at Long Branch, N.J., July 2nd and Saratoga, N.Y., July 16, 1872," Currier & Ives, c. 1872. (Library of Congress)

and almost embraced one another; ladies, though half alarmed at the torrent of excitement, waved their handkerchiefs and parasols."[36] But enthusiasm was dampened when the crowd noticed Longfellow limping as the horses returned to their handlers in front of the grandstand.

As Morrissey had first noticed, something was terribly wrong with the horse. The metal racing shoe on his left front foot had bent in half and injured his sole. Initial journalistic prognostications that he would never run again proved correct, though he did go on to have a noteworthy career as a stallion, siring, among a host of stakes winners, two Kentucky Derby champions. Despite the unfortunate end to Longfellow's racing career, the gallantry that the big brown horse had shown in defeat, along with Harry Bassett's brilliant performance in victory, caused the

117

Times to opine, "Never, perhaps, in the racing history of the Saratoga or any other track, has such a scene been witnessed as took place today."[37]

On the meet's final day, the featured race was the inaugural running of the Alabama Stakes, named, in a roundabout way, for an English-born Confederate veteran. As a teenager, in 1841, Captain William Cottrill moved to Mobile, Alabama, and joined his brother-in-law's butcher business. Their operation was sufficiently successful to allow Cottrill to begin breeding and racing Thoroughbreds. Following the Civil War, in which he commanded an independent cavalry company, Cottrill was one of the first horsemen of the Deep South to race his horses at the top new racing venues in the North, including Saratoga, Jerome Park, and Monmouth. He quickly won the respect of northern racing leaders, including Morrissey, and an offer was made for a stakes race to be named in Cottrill's honor at Saratoga. Too modest to be comfortable with a race explicitly named for him, Cottrill accepted a compromise of sorts and suggested that the race be called the Alabama. Today it is the second-oldest event run at Saratoga and is among the most prestigious races for three-year-old fillies in America. Southerners had been an important element of the Saratoga social scene before the Civil War, and the return of leading southern horsemen following the end of the conflict was instrumental in cementing the track's national stature. Thus a race named for a state that had been in rebellion less than a decade earlier was appropriate, if unusual.[38]

The first running of the Alabama "was, to the Southern element, like a bad headache after a severe midnight's debauch," the *New York Times* reported. Southerners had heavily supported a filly owned by Colonel McDaniel, but she was defeated by August Belmont's filly Woodbine. The event capped off another successful race meet for Morrissey at Saratoga and further illustrated the growing appeal of horse racing, which was crossing divides of geography and social class.[39]

At the conclusion of the meet the *Nashville Union and American* declared, "All appearances indicate that Morrissey is the leading gamester of the Western world, both in money, self-restraint, individual character and force, and in completeness of his establishment."[40] By that time Morrissey's casino was the most famous in America, he was leasing the racetrack from the Saratoga Association, and he had firmly established the Saratoga race meet as a high point on American sporting and social calendars. But Morrissey knew that there was still potential for growth within Saratoga's sporting scene.[41]

The following year he offered to pay the expenses of the fledgling Intercollegiate Regatta, the national championship of the Rowing Association of American Colleges, if the association (the first intercollegiate athletic organization in America) would hold its national championships at Saratoga Lake. A year earlier, Morrissey had organized and hosted the Saratoga International Regatta, billed as a world championship race for four-man rowing crews, at Saratoga Lake. The Ward brothers from Poughkeepsie, New York, took the $2,000 first prize in a record-setting performance over the four-mile course, defeating top professional teams from both sides of the Atlantic. Rowing was among the most popular sports in America, and the thousands of fans in attendance for Morrissey's regatta saw a race that the *New York Times* called "the grandest aquatic event ever witnessed in America."[42] But Morrissey's bid to host a *collegiate* event set off torrid debate in the pages of the nation's sporting journals regarding the propriety of amateur athletes competing in a den of sin like Saratoga. To the great relief of his critics, Morrissey's initial pitch for the 1873 Intercollegiate Regatta was rejected, and the event was held, for the third straight year, in Massachusetts.

That fall Morrissey instead held an independent amateur race at Saratoga Lake. He banned auction pools in the vicinity of the lake in order to demonstrate that it could be done, and in hopes that his bid to host the collegians the following year might be looked upon more favorably. The *Boston Daily Advertiser* sneered at his efforts: "It will be an unfortunate day for the interests of college contests when mercenary considerations have a prominent place in the preparation for them. If the students cannot afford to pay their own expenses with such assistance as the friends of college sports willingly contribute as an encouragement, not as speculation, regattas ought to be discontinued. Nobody of discretion doubts that the prime motive of Mr. Morrissey, in wishing to bring the contest to Saratoga, is to make the students serve his gambling speculations, precisely as the horses do who run on his race course there."[43]

The *Advertiser* was correct in surmising that Morrissey hoped to profit from the event, but the newspaper failed to recognize the wider potential of big-time sports that Morrissey saw. Although some critics feared that Morrissey wanted the rowers to contest their national championships in Saratoga so that his casino might capitalize on a few days of increased tourist traffic in the area, Morrissey was never interested in luring the rowers or their schoolmates into his casino. He had a broader vision and understood that enhancing Saratoga's stature by making it the preeminent site of championship sporting events would have ramifications far beyond a day or a week of competition. Morrissey knew that his own fortunes would rise with those of the town in the long term if he could develop and enhance Saratoga's reputation as a sporting center, and in early 1874 the Rowing Association of American Colleges announced an agreement to hold its fourth annual regatta on Saratoga Lake that summer.

One newspaper whined, "Saratoga is, during the summer, headquarters of American blacklegs. There rules Hon. John Morrissey, M.C., in royal state; and thither to his gambling halls and to the races gather in annual pilgrimage all the jockeys and sharpers in the country; and thither were invited and thither have agreed to go the crews of the college regatta. It is an outrage and a disgrace. It is impossible to separate Saratoga from John Morrissey and his blacklegs. It is they that have captured the witless representatives of what had been our honest sport."[44] The fears and objections of those opposed to Saratoga as a host site seem remarkably quaint to a modern ear until one remembers that the National Collegiate Athletic Association still refuses to allow Las Vegas to host the men's basketball championship tournament, and none of the major American sports leagues have dared to locate a franchise there, despite every indication that such a move could be profitable.

Not all journalistic bloviating on the subject was opposed to Saratoga and Morrissey, however. An editorial in *Forest and Stream,* a sporting magazine published in New York City, opined:

> The moral objections urged against Saratoga are not supported by the facts. Some are worthless, others are absurd. That John Morrissey is the proprietor of a gambling establishment must be admitted; but that it is free of access to anyone, that it invites visitors, must be denied. It is not a public gambling house, but a private clubhouse, very difficult [to] access. It is well nigh impossible for a young man to gain admission there, much less a college student. John Morrissey is a very shrewd man, and he knows very well that should any college student be fleeced in his rooms, the hostility already existing in Saratoga against him would be fanned to such a breeze that he would be compelled to give up his business completely.[45]

Morrissey assured skeptics that no college-aged patrons would be allowed in his casino, and he made sure that no horse racing would be conducted during regatta week. Instead, a series of other collegiate sporting events were scheduled, including baseball games and footraces. City leaders pledged that there would be "no pool-selling, that moderate fixed rates should be charged by hotel keepers and hack-drivers, and that 'for this occasion only' Saratoga should be as innocent as Paradise before the advent of snakes."[46]

As the town excitedly prepared for the biggest American sporting spectacle of the summer, the *New York Times* reported, "The public interest has been aroused in this race to a very uncommon extent. We can scarcely remember an event not involving a war, or some vast issue in politics, which has occasioned so much excitement." The *Chicago Inter Ocean* declared, "Never since the beginning of Saratoga's history as a watering place has the city been so crowded as today by the multitudes which have poured in from all directions. The sidewalks are crowded to almost impassibility, and no place could be livelier, and brighter, and gayer than Saratoga is today." Some twenty-five thousand visitors, including competitors, students, and alumni from nine schools—Harvard, Yale, Columbia, Williams, Princeton, Wesleyan, Dartmouth, Cornell, and Trinity—crowded into town. Despite the organizers' best efforts to exclude them, or at least to minimize their visibility, gamblers made their way to Saratoga in time for the race, with many gravitating toward Yale and Harvard in the prerace semi-clandestine auction pools.[47]

On Saturday morning, after a two-day delay attributed to weather (those with a bent toward conspiracy noted that such delays were good for local business), spectators made their way to the lake by whatever means they could. A Chicago newspaper observed that "hay wagons, delivery wagons, road wagons, carriages, omnibuses, carryalls, ox-carts, milk-carts, cabbage-carts, dirt-carts, and all other available and conceivable vehicles were pressed into service by the persistent sight-seers."[48] Shortly before 11:00 a.m. the starting gun was fired and the nine crews were off. Columbia started quickly and remained in front for most of the first mile. Harvard eased ahead briefly, but Columbia soon regained the lead, leaving Harvard and its archrivals from Yale to battle for second position in what soon became a three-boat race. Entering the final mile, Yale had poked its bow in front of Harvard's, but the two boats were traveling close together and collided. Yale emerged from the incident with a broken rudder and was out of contention. (At the conclusion of the race the two teams made reciprocal claims of foul, both of which were ultimately disallowed.) Columbia maintained its lead for the final mile and completed the three-mile course eight seconds ahead of Wesleyan, which had made a late move to finish four seconds in front of third-place Harvard.

"People of every sex and age followed the boat's course along the marshy turf at a run, and reached the landing stage just in time to meet Columbia's prow as it touched," the *Inter Ocean* reported. "The crew leaped in the water, beseeched their boat, and fell into the arms of their college chums, who stood ready to receive them." Upon reaching the shore, Columbia's captain dramatically fainted and was "taken to the hotel on the shoulders of his friends."[49]

The swarming crowds followed the crews downtown for postrace celebration and sorrow-drowning, creating quite a scene on the streets, where "men jumped up and down, danced, shrieked, yelled, threw their hats, tore their coats, and gave vent to their uncontrollable excitement in the maddest manner." Harvard students and alumni, happy to have defeated Yale, joined in Columbia's celebration. They hired a marching band and together they rambled through the streets and hotel lobbies, cheering at the sight of their schools' colors in various windows, yelling school cheers, and "weeping on each other's bosoms. It was very jolly and very crazy." In New York City, crowds lingered at the newspaper offices eagerly awaiting the results, and the *New York Times* office was inundated with hundreds of telegraph messages from curious sports fans across the country.[50]

Despite the controversial weather delays and complaints about high prices, Saratoga received favorable reviews for its handling of the event. The *Times* acknowledged that the regatta "was probably the finest spectacle of the sort ever seen on American waters . . . [and] it is doubtful if in the whole country a better field could be found for a regatta than Saratoga Lake." Historian

Edward Hotaling has called the regatta, and the national attention that accompanied it, "the birth of intercollegiate sports on the modern scale—and the country's greatest sporting event of any kind [to that time]."[51]

Saratoga had attracted tourists for decades, but Morrissey had managed in a relatively short time to transform the area into a sporting mecca. The next year's regatta attracted three new teams and record crowds, and Morrissey kept his clubhouse open throughout the week. Cornell, a school barely a decade old, won the 1875 regatta in what was, through the end of the century, widely held by aficionados as the greatest collegiate rowing race ever contested. The Cornell team repeated as champion the following year at Saratoga, when the town also welcomed the championship track-and-field meet for the Athletic Association of American Colleges. The meet, which was the first official intercollegiate championship of its kind, was held at a small trotting course just outside of town at Glen Mitchell.[52]

From the modest start of a small Thoroughbred race meet in 1863, by the mid-1870s Morrissey had clearly demonstrated the economic clout of major sporting events. He had risen to the forefront of the developing American sports landscape by staging championships that attracted the interest of the moneyed set, as well as average folk, gamblers, and sporting purists. The leading financiers of the era were comfortable in the opulence of his Club House, and his race meet drew America's top horses and horsemen each summer. But his sporting events were enthusiastically supported by the middle classes as well, and he was shrewd enough to placate the fears of all but the most virulent opponents of gambling and gamblers.

By staging events that appealed to a broad swath of Americans, Morrissey achieved an unprecedented stature within American sports. While there were still many who turned up well-bred noses at an Irish pugilist-gambler, he had become fluent in the ways and language of the upper crust. Morrissey's rise from humble beginnings served as an affirmation of the promise of America, and his name and reputation still carried great weight within the New York underworld thanks to memories of his fistic successes both in and out of the prize ring. Morrissey's ability to operate in a variety of social and economic spheres was also an important part of what made him a very effective politician. And within New York political circles in the 1870s, there was still no one more influential than John Morrissey.

7

Vindication

With the defeat of the Morrissey-led Young Democracy in the spring of 1870, Boss Tweed and his Tammany cronies had been left to run amok in New York City, accelerating an unprecedented period of municipal pilfer. The following summer a series of articles appearing in the *New York Times* exposed many of the Tweed Ring's misdeeds and eventually helped put a stop to the pillaging, but not before the grafters had made away with tens of millions of public dollars. Estimations of the plunder ran as high as $200 million, though more reasonable guesses placed the amount at closer to $50 million.

It was common practice at the time for contractors to inflate invoices sent to the city by 15 percent, which allowed Tweed and his allies to skim directly off the top of any municipal outlay. Some of the more egregious examples of fraud exposed by the *Times* included $5.6 million in expenditures for furniture and carpets, $41,000 for "brooms, etc.," and $404,000 for safes in the courthouse, an edifice that cost $13 million to build (on an original budget of $250,000), almost twice the amount the United States paid for Alaska in 1867.[1]

In the elections of 1871 the Tweed Ring was nearly completely destroyed, with the notable exception of Boss Tweed himself, who was reelected to the state senate. But Tweed was soon

William M. Tweed (1823–1878) led the most notoriously corrupt regime in the history of American municipal government. Morrissey helped lead a failed revolt against the Tweed Ring in 1870 and rose to power upon Tweed's subsequent fall from grace.

prosecuted for his crimes and would die in prison. The Boss's demise left a power vacuum within New York City politics that was filled by "Honest" John Kelly, a son of Irish immigrants born in New York City in 1822. Like Tweed, Kelly had begun his political rise as a young man in the volunteer fire department. He advanced through the local political ranks and served two terms in Congress in the 1850s before being appointed sheriff. His pay in that office consisted entirely of fees he collected, and it was as sheriff that Kelly earned the flippant nickname "Honest John." His dishonesty eventually caught up with him, and he was accused of overcharging constituents by some $30,000. He retired from his position as sheriff to run for mayor, but when he did not receive Tammany's backing, he embarked on an extended sightseeing tour of Europe and the Holy Land, returning in time to take advantage of the Tweed Ring's fall.

In 1874 Kelly helped to elect the Tammany candidate for mayor of New York City, businessman William H. Wickham. John Morrissey had returned to the Tammany fold in the upheaval created by Tweed's downfall and had also backed Wickham for mayor. Upon paying Wickham a visit at City Hall early in his mayoral tenure, Morrissey was stopped at the door by a fancily attired attendant who haughtily stated that His Honor the Mayor had issued instructions that he was not to be disturbed. Taken aback, Morrissey instructed the attendant to "give my compliments to His Honor Mayor Wickham and ask him to tell Billy Wickham that when John Morrissey has time to put on French airs, he may call again."

Days later, a friend saw Morrissey passing through the park near the mayor's office. Morrissey was uncharacteristically dressed in a swallowtail coat, patent leather boots, and white kid gloves. A light overcoat was draped over one forearm, and in the other hand he carried a thick book. The friend asked Morrissey if he was on his way to a wedding. "No," Morrissey answered, "I've just bought a French dictionary to help me talk to our dandy mayor. I'm going in full dress to make a call, for that is now the style at the Hotel Wickham. No Irish need apply now." When Morrissey was finally allowed to see the mayor, they shared a laugh over the whole matter, but they would soon have a falling out related to the larger fracture within the ranks of the Tweedless Tammany Democrats.[2]

Kelly had a serious thirst for power, and by 1873 New York newspapers were referring to him as "Boss Kelly." But Morrissey also held serious political clout, especially among the working classes, and some observers identified Morrissey, not Kelly, as the chief power broker in New York. The *New York Times* declared, "John Morrissey is the admitted autocrat of Tammany. Whatever is done by Tammany is, in fact, done by Morrissey. Whatever morality Tammany may have is Morrissey's in reality. He has succeeded in pushing even John Kelly aside, and has stepped into Tweed's place. Tammany must always have a master, and Morrissey is the new 'boss.'"[3] Following the 1873 elections an editorial observed: "Who controls the Democratic Party of this State?

Tammany Hall. And who controls Tammany Hall? John Morrissey. And who won the elections in this City? John Morrissey and Tammany."[4]

Morrissey and Kelly shared power awkwardly for more than a year, but in the late spring of 1875 the former allies parted ways. The nominal reason was Morrissey's opposition to the reduction in city laborers' wages advocated by Kelly and his supporters. But the rift actually stemmed from Kelly's belief that Morrissey stood in the way of Kelly's political ambitions and Morrissey's belief that Kelly had failed to satisfactorily back one of Morrissey's friends as a candidate for a minor elected office. In June the Tammany Committee on Discipline issued a preliminary report to the General Committee, concluding that Morrissey had "subverted the harmony which should prevail among the faithful."[5] The committee added a final insult by declaring Morrissey's seat on the General Committee vacant, effectively ostracizing him from the party.[6]

Talk of the Democratic schism could be heard all over New York, but Morrissey escaped the ruckus for the start of the racing season at Saratoga. When he returned to Manhattan at the end of the summer, support was building for him to run for a seat in the New York state senate, in Boss Tweed's old district. The *Times* reported that Morrissey wanted to take his time before issuing any statements, but "judging from his demeanor and emphatic language, [Morrissey] has come back with the intention of making a vigorous fight with Kelly for supremacy in Tammany Hall."[7] In October Morrissey was unanimously nominated for the state senate by the anti-Tammany Democrats, who issued a stirring statement urging his acceptance. "Principles of vital importance are at stake," the group declared. "Not only are the rights of the people at issue, but the very foundation of Democracy itself is shaken and endangered."[8]

At first Morrissey politely declined the nomination, but his supporters ignored his nominal wishes and began to hang cam-

Along with John Morrissey, "Honest" John Kelly (1822–1886) filled the power vacuum in New York politics created by the Tweed Ring's demise in the 1870s. Kelly and Morrissey shared power briefly, but a rift between the two motivated Morrissey to again run for elected office in 1875. (Library of Congress)

paign posters around the district. Addressing his supporters in a letter published in local papers, Morrissey acceded to their demands for his acceptance of their nomination:

> My duty to the cause which you represent demands that I should no longer refuse my active cooperation, and if, as I verily believe, the result shall be the downfall of the dictatorship which threatens to enthrall for an indefinite period the Democratic voters of New York, and the vindications of the rights of free and honest labor; and if, as a part of this result, I shall be chosen to the important and distinguished office of Senator, I shall endeavor so to discharge my duties as to merit in some degree the confidence which you have been pleased to express in supporting me for that office.[9]

Morrissey's opponent in the election was the incumbent, John Fox, a comrade in the failed Young Democracy movement who returned to Tammany's inner circles after Tweed's downfall and would remain a Tammany stalwart until his death in 1914.

The Fourth District election received more journalistic attention than any that year and was a popular subject for barroom banter. In at least one case the banter turned bloody. At the Fifth Avenue Hotel, a man named Edwin Haggerty, who had achieved notoriety by burglarizing a City Hall office building, shot a middling Tammany politician named Ferris, who had offered to bet Haggerty $1,000 that Morrissey would lose the election.

"You're no good; you have no money to bet," Haggerty responded.

"If we were on the street, you [would] dare not say so," Ferris replied.

"Yes I would," Haggerty said.

"Come on then," Ferris challenged. Once they were outside, Haggerty drew a revolver and shot Ferris "through the scrotum."[10]

Morrissey had the broad support of the working classes, but he was also backed by friends in the financial sector, who had found him to be trustworthy in his business dealings. Many on Wall Street recalled Morrissey's run of bad luck in stock speculation a couple of years earlier, when he had run up debts some estimated to be as high as $300,000. Although it was widely assumed that he would never be able to repay those obligations, he had paid back every dollar within a year. As a result, he was given access to as much money as he needed to conduct his brief election campaign.[11]

The *Times,* which had often been critical of Morrissey, came out in favor of his candidacy. "John Morrissey is a blunt man, of excellent practical sense, who is incapable of making sham pretenses or deceiving his friends," the paper explained. "When Morrissey was in Congress, who ever accused him of taking bribes, or otherwise betraying the trust?" As for John Fox, the newspaper opined, "Like all small tyrants, he is ready to grind the faces of the working men into the dust. A worse or more dangerous candidate could hardly be presented to the public. Let the people of the Fourth District treat him as he deserves, for he is emphatically a bad man to elect. Do not vote for him."[12]

Morrissey spent the week before the election making appearances all over lower Manhattan. He regularly reiterated that his "treason" with respect to Tammany was justified. "I want nothing from Tammany Hall," Morrissey told a group of working-class supporters at a packed assembly hall. "I fought my battle in Tammany Hall and was thrown out. . . . This issue is between the poorer classes and the aristocrats. If you are defeated now you will be beaten for life. It is not a question of men, but of principles."[13]

He went on to draw parallels between his boxing career and the political realm, reminding his supporters that with their help he would win the "fight" against Fox. Barroom gamblers shared his confidence, making Morrissey the solid betting favor-

Even as he refashioned himself as a reformer in his campaigns for the New York state senate, Morrissey was often harshly depicted as a menacing brute in the political press. "Putting a Head On," *Harper's Weekly*, September 26, 1876.

ite to win the election. New Yorkers knew that the prediction of election results could be a tricky matter given the city's record of pervasive voting fraud, but the *Times* predicted that such chicanery would not be a problem in the Fourth District race, as Morrissey's group knew "as much as there is to be known on the subject, and the votes cast will be effectual and determinative."[14]

The day before the election, John Fox's team sent men to taverns to buy drinks for potential voters in a desperate attempt to round up late support. On Election Day Morrissey "marched his men to the polls, in squads of five to twenty," early in the morning and "got in his votes before the Fox money could come into play." Restaurant owners, hotel operators, and other employers friendly to the Morrissey campaign instructed their employees to head to the polls and vote for Morrissey. Despite widespread reports of attempted vote buying by Fox, and after a campaign of only eleven days, Morrissey was elected by a majority of 3,500.[15]

Morrissey proved to be a much more active legislator in Albany than he had been in Washington, championing the causes of laborers and law enforcement, supporting financing mechanisms for urban improvements, and voting to consolidate parts of the bloated New York City government. But the most significant political event of Morrissey's first year in Albany was the presidential election, which would be the most controversial in American history. At their April convention, New York Democrats nominated New York governor Samuel J. Tilden for president. Morrissey's relationship with Tilden had been mixed at best, but because John Kelly had become a vocal opponent of Tilden, Morrissey jumped on his bandwagon.

Morrissey and a group of anti-Tammany New York Democrats traveled to the Democratic national convention in St. Louis in order to support their candidate. Tilden received his party's nomination, while the Republicans tapped Ohio governor Rutherford B. Hayes at their convention in Cincinnati. In the November elections Tilden received 250,000 more votes than Hayes, but there were problems with the election results in Florida, South Carolina, Oregon, and Louisiana, where accusations of vote fraud were rampant.

Rumors of Morrissey's involvement in presidential election chicanery soon emerged. While he later confirmed that two men from Louisiana had indeed traveled to New York to offer their electoral votes to Tilden for $1 million, Morrissey claimed that he turned them down. "I could have gotten the votes for $50,000," he explained. Yet he insisted that he had not accepted such an offer because "I wouldn't cross the street to make Tilden president that way. He's ungrateful and deceiving, and if it had come out he would have denied all knowledge of it, and thrown all the odium on me."[16]

A fifteen-person electoral commission ultimately decided the election in favor of Hayes, whose first significant act as president was to return home rule to the former Confederacy, ending Reconstruction.[17] Morrissey had taken more than $300,000 in bets on the election (some claimed that the number had been far higher), and in December, as uncertainty regarding the results still loomed, he announced that all bets were off. At first he was inclined to keep his commission on the stakes money that he had held, but after vociferous condemnation in the press, he decided to return all funds.[18]

Newspapers were critical of the manner in which Morrissey had facilitated wagering on the election, but both Morrissey and his family had become accustomed to disparagement from the national press. Although their personal lives were much less scrutinized than they had been when Morrissey was a congressman, the occasional article still appeared in the New York newspapers. Earlier that summer the *New York Times* had published descriptions of a lavish twenty-first birthday party for Morrissey's son, Johnny, held at the Morrissey residence in Saratoga, where young Morrissey was given presents that included a deed to property valued at $10,000, a diamond-encrusted locket, and $1,000 in silver. American newspaper readers had been introduced to John Jr. three years earlier when he nearly killed himself while lighting "powder snakes" made of gunpowder. According to a report in the *Saratoga Sentinel,* while on a hunting trip in the Adirondacks, the young man was "playing in the morning with powder, laying trains from a three pound canister and exploding them. He undertook to pour some on a piece of cotton, which, unknown to him, was on fire." The resultant explosion, which was heard some four miles away, set his clothes on fire, "but his colored attendant, with presence of mind, tore the burning clothing off and threw a quilt over him to smother the flames." Johnny had survived that adventure thanks to his attendant (named Atkins) and a hurried trip to the doctor, but he had never been in great health, and less than five months after his twenty-first birthday he was dead. One newspaper attributed the young man's demise to "diseased lungs"; others claimed that he had Bright's disease, the catchall term for a variety of kidney ailments that his father had been treated for while on hiatus from his congressional duties, though no one was quite sure of the cause of the young man's fatal malady. His shattered parents were at his bedside when he passed away.[19]

An obituary appearing in the *New York Tribune* described him as "a young man of very quiet habits, a little inclined to reserve, and filled with an ambition to excel in literary pursuits. He had all the frank and manly qualities of his father—qualities which all who know Morrissey recognize—and with a refinement of manner and culture of mind which the father did not possess." John Morrissey was devastated by the loss of his only child. "The father lived largely in and for the boy," the *Tribune* explained.[20] Morrissey probably never fully recovered from Johnny's death, but he plowed ahead with his political activity. He had already achieved far more in terms of wealth, fame, and power than he ever could have reasonably hoped, yet he continued to be dogged by critics' mumbled suggestions that his electoral victories had been a result of his gangland connections, with the implicit accusation that he would not have been able to win a political race in a more "civilized" district.

In the fall of 1877 Morrissey was presented with an opportunity to combat those lingering perceptions when the anti-Tammany Democrats from the Seventh District nominated him for the New York senate. Known as the "silk stockings district" because it encompassed a number of affluent East Side neighborhoods, the Seventh also included John Kelly's home precinct, which made the idea of victory there especially appealing to Morrissey. When the Seventh District Republicans also nominated

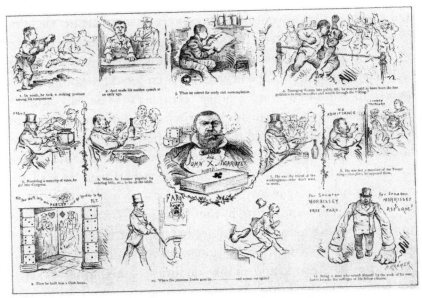

Despite his having served two terms as a U.S. congressman, Morrissey's political opponents continued to publicize his checkered past. Peter Kramer (1823–1907), c. 1877, originally published in *Puck* magazine. (Library of Congress)

him, Morrissey decided to run, declaring, "I want to beat [Kelly] on his own stoop."[21]

Accepting the nominations, Morrissey promised to protect the interests of laborers, schoolteachers, policemen, and firemen against those of "useless officials with an insatiable greed for office, position, and place."[22] To oppose Morrissey, the Tammany Democrats nominated Augustus Schell, the grand sachem of Tammany Hall. Derided by Morrissey supporters as "a wise-looking owl-like figurehead to preside at John Kelly's meetings," Schell was a corporate lawyer, a board member of the powerful New York Central Railroad, and the former chairman of the Democratic National Committee.[23]

In his short campaign Morrissey stuck to the proworker, anti-Tammany message that had helped him win his previous election. He legitimately claimed a record of success in Albany, including helping to pass a series of laws that brought some improved efficiency and reduced redundancy to various governmental departments. Morrissey promised to continue to look out for the interests of the working classes without alienating the wealthy by reminding the upper classes that if workers' wages fell too low, they would be unable to pay their rents.[24]

Just as there had been in Morrissey's previous elections, there were multiple reports of violence stemming from political arguments related to Morrissey's candidacy as Election Day approached. For example, at a saloon on Thirty-First Street and Fourth Avenue (modern-day Park Avenue), a group of railroad workers were drinking and discussing politics. Opinions differed as to whether Morrissey or Schell would win. After a Morrissey supporter loudly expressed his intention to vote for the former champion, a Schell man responded, "You can't vote, you've been ten days on the island [in prison] out of the last thirty." The Morrissey partisan threatened to "pull the man's ears," at which point the proprietor of the establishment told the men to take their discussion outside. The Morrissey devotee returned a short time later and "drank considerably." In the meantime, the Schell supporter was discovered lying in the street and was taken first to the police station and then on to the hospital, where he died the following day from a fractured skull.[25]

As the election campaign neared its conclusion, Morrissey was having trouble getting out of bed, suffering from what was thought to be a lingering cold that he had been battling since early October.[26] Four days before the election Morrissey was receiving visitors and supporters in his suite at the Ashland House hotel on Twenty-Fourth Street near Fourth Avenue, where he had established a campaign headquarters. The following day he left his sick bed to speak to an overflowing crowd at the Germania Assembly Hall on Twenty-Sixth Street and Seventh Avenue. Arriving at the building, he "forced his way slowly through the throng,

THE NOTORIOUS JOHN MORRISSEY

amid deafening cheers and cries of welcome from throats that persisted as if they would never tire. The cheering extended into the hall and was maintained until Morrissey reached the platform." He spoke respectfully of Schell personally, but went on to say that "he had come into the district to beat John Kelly, and Augustus Schell as his representative." Morrissey proudly touted his record in Albany, recounted his successes as a prizefighter, and concluded his remarks with a challenge to the voters to win the election fight for him. From there he went straight to a rally on Fourth Avenue before returning to his room, exhausted.[27]

Morrissey felt much better the following day and made four public appearances that night. At his first stop, on Avenue A, Jefferson Hall "was crammed almost to suffocation," and he had to squirm through the crowd to reach the stage. The *New York Times* reported: "His voice was husky, but a profound silence suddenly fell upon the rough men who a moment before had been so boisterous, and they listened to the brief speech with close attention, only interrupting him by applause and outspoken approval." He made three more appearances that night, addressing wildly enthusiastic crowds. Back at his headquarters, he told friends, "Kelly must beat me or I will beat him. If he lets me get back to the legislature for two years, I will have him out of the Controller's office before the 1st of May. Don't make any mistake about it."[28]

The day before the election Morrissey issued a statement, in which he complained of dirty tactics by his opponent's campaign team:

Whatever of folly or of wrong-doing these assailants may ascribe to my youth, I have earnestly tried to atone for in my manhood. With my whole life known and laid bare to the people of the community, they have three times honored me with their confidence in elevating me to public offices of trust. Let my slanderers turn their prejudices and poison to my record in every office I have

140

Morrissey in his later years.

held. If they can demonstrate that I have ever forfeited my word or violated a pledge made to the people, or that any act of mine bears the impress of dishonesty or deceit, I shall bow to such record and admit the justice of their attack; if not, I shall ask my constituents and supporters to condemn this unseemly and unmanly method of assault intended but to misguide the people and arouse their prejudice against me.[29]

Still debilitated by illness, and exhausted from campaigning, Morrissey remained inside his headquarters on Election Day. Tammany Hall had a far greater presence on the streets and around the precincts than Morrissey's ragtag operation, but the voting proceeded relatively peacefully and without major incident. Most of the ballots were cast by late morning, which left the afternoon for campaign staffs to drag stragglers to the polls. Schell's team widely distributed cigars and whiskey, but many recipients of the gifts voted for Morrissey anyway. Tammany agents made a late push for African American votes with promises of "favors," but Morrissey had broad support from black voters, along with white Republicans and various other groups who were tired of Tammany. By 7:00 p.m. John Kelly had conceded the race on Schell's behalf, acknowledging a comfortable two-thousand-vote win for Morrissey.[30]

At Morrissey's headquarters, with few exceptions, only his doctor and close friends had been allowed to see him all day. But at 10:00 p.m. the physician gave approval for a newspaper reporter to speak to the victorious candidate, who was noticeably sweaty and wrapped in a blanket and a shawl. "Didn't I tell you I'd carry Kelly's own district?" Morrissey asked the reporter, before proceeding to a less-than-humble assessment of the election, which, he noted, had "hardly been a fair fight on Kelly's part, with all the power, with all the money and patronage of the district at his command, with money distributed through all the liquor stores, and coercion of all the party men, it was not a manly

Morrissey won his final electoral victory in New York's fashionable Seventh Senatorial District, quieting critics who claimed that Morrissey's prior political success had been achieved as a result of gangland connections. This cartoon shows the aristocrats of the Seventh District bowing in reverence to Senator Morrissey.

thing on Kelly's part. If I had been well I would have beaten him by 7,500 votes."[31]

The *Christian Union* evinced a common equivocal perspective in explaining that "thousands voted for [Morrissey] simply because they preferred to send a professional gambler to represent honest political principles rather than a professional politician to represent the most disreputable political organization in the whole country."[32] Journalists had employed a tone of repulsed curiosity mixed with begrudging respect to describe Morrissey throughout his political career. But even his most vocal critics had to concede that he had achieved legitimate success and wielded real power.

The morning after his election victory, Morrissey managed to sneak out of his room and walk down to a favorite spot for breakfast. As he finished a light meal at the Hoffman House, his physician, who had found Morrissey missing when he went to check on his patient, stormed in and chastised him for going outside in his condition. The doctor called a carriage and helped the senator to it. Morrissey tried to convince the driver to take him through the park, but he could win only a compromise trip to its entrance before returning to his headquarters, where he rested for most of the day. That night five thousand people gathered in the street below Morrissey's room, and the festivities included a brass band, fireworks, and singing. The crowd demanded an appearance by their triumphant candidate, but they were to be disappointed. Susie Morrissey appeared on the balcony to acknowledge the gathering and opened her window so that she and her friends could listen to the celebration, but John was too sick to address the crowd himself on the cool November night. He sent a deputy to thank his supporters and to tell them, "Mr. Morrissey was prouder of the victory he had won than he would be to be President of the United States."[33]

His physician decided that Morrissey should travel south in order to remove himself from "the severe bleak weather common in this latitude in November, and away from associations who would be apt to fatigue him by conversation on exciting topics." Morrissey told only a few friends of his travel plans, and some of them came with Susie—who would join her husband later—to the wharf to say good-bye. A newspaper reporter asked Morrissey if he would return in time to attend the opening of the legislature. "Oh, I'll be there, if I'm alive," Morrissey replied. He traveled first to Savannah, then on to Jacksonville.[34]

His health took a turn for the worse early in the new year, and the *Times* began publishing daily reports on Morrissey's condition, which seemed to fluctuate wildly. On January 16 the newspaper reported that "Mr. John Morrissey is quite comfortable tonight, and all immediate danger is believed to be past." The following day, however, "Mr. Morrissey's condition was exceedingly low, and there is no change for the better tonight. His mind last night and this morning was somewhat wandering at times.

Following his 1877 election victory, Morrissey snuck out, against his doctor's orders, for breakfast at the Hoffman House (pictured here c. 1890). "Interior View of the Hoffman House Bar," H. A. Thomas & Wylie. (Library of Congress)

He has today given his wife full directions in regard to closing up his business." His maladies were described as Bright's disease and disease of the heart, but the brutal lifestyle of his younger days could just as easily have been listed among the causes of his ailment, as it was exceedingly rare for fighters of Morrissey's generation to reach a fiftieth birthday. He was visited by a priest, and his doctor told a reporter that "unless there was a change for the better inside of 48 hours there would be no use of a change."[35] But Morrissey's strength gradually improved, and by the following week the *Times* was reporting on its front page that he "slept seven hours in bed last night and ate quite heartily today."[36] After another setback in mid-March, Morrissey was deemed well enough to travel and was back in New York by the end of the month.

Finding the barrage of friends and well-wishers in New York burdensome, Morrissey, accompanied by his wife, soon headed north again, first to Troy for a couple of weeks and then on to Saratoga, where he took a room at the newly constructed Adelphi Hotel. He continued to keep abreast of the political news from Albany, and his friends maintained hope that Morrissey could regain his strength. But he suffered a stroke at the end of April that left him paralyzed on his right side, and he never recovered. He told the *New York Daily Tribune,* "I'm running neck and neck with death and rapidly tiring."[37] On May 1 he weakened after reading an afternoon newspaper and died at 7:30 that evening surrounded by his wife, a few friends, and a priest.[38]

At the New York legislature the following day, Morrissey's seat was decorated with flowers, and the senate adopted a series of resolutions in Morrissey's memory: "Resolved: That the Senate has heard with profound emotion of the death of our late associate, Hon. John Morrissey. Resolved: That we desire to certify our respect for the remarkable qualities of the deceased—for his individuality of character, for his great moral courage, for his devotion to principle and to his friends, for the persistent energy which marked his life-long struggle against formidable obstacles, and above all, for his rare and unquestioned integrity."[39]

Hundreds of mourners came from twilight to midnight to pay their respects in the parlor rooms of the Adelphi. The next day the casket was placed on a train bound for Troy, and crowds filled the stations at each stop to express their sympathies. Well-wishers gathered at Susie's mother's house, where she and John had been married twenty-four years earlier. A small service was conducted in the living room the next morning after which friends and family proceeded to St. Peter's Church and finally to the cemetery, where Morrissey was interred between his father and his son, beneath a stately obelisk.

The *National Police Gazette* encapsulated sentiments expressed in obituaries across the country when it asserted, "Few public men of our day have arisen from beginnings so discouraging to a place so high in the general esteem of the community, or experienced such vicissitudes as the dead senator."[40] Morrissey had been widely presumed to be a millionaire, and he had, on multiple occasions, won and lost sizable fortunes. But much of his wealth was in real estate that was heavily encumbered by mortgages, and he left a relatively modest estate, for which William Travers served as an executor. On opening day at the racetrack that summer, the *Times* observed, "Everybody misses the stalwart form of Morrissey, and even the staid and religious portion of the community, who had no sympathy with his calling, admit that his death has left a void which cannot easily be filled. As a racing disciplinarian he was without rival, and the reputation of the Saratoga course attests to his capacity as a manager. Those whom he has left to manage the track have only to move in the rut that Morrissey marked out to be successful."[41]

As an athlete, a promoter, and a proprietor, Morrissey participated in and contributed to some of the most significant sporting events of the nineteenth century. Up to that time, no one had done more to develop the commodification and commercialization of sports in America. But Morrissey was soon to be all but forgotten as organizers of sport—continually dogged by the reform-minded—sought to distance themselves and their sports from the world that Morrissey had once inhabited.

Gamblers Albert Spencer and Charles Reed, who had acquired ownership interests in the Saratoga racetrack and Club House casino during Morrissey's lifetime, took control of both upon Morrissey's death, with Spencer focusing on the casino and Reed on the racing. Spencer took on Richard Canfield as a partner in the casino in 1883 and sold the facility and business to him the following year. Canfield ran the casino successfully until 1907, when he finally gave in to antigambling opposition and shut down the operation. Four years later he sold the structure to the city, which has preserved the historic building; its former grounds are now part of Congress Park.

In 1923 Walter S. Vosburgh published an "official" history of American Thoroughbred racing for The Jockey Club, which was then the governing body for New York racing (it remains the keeper of the registry of Thoroughbreds in America). Modeled after the English Jockey Club, the American version, founded in 1894, was as influential a group as there was in American racing. Vosburgh's *Racing in America, 1866–1921* became the foundation for subsequent histories of the sport, but nowhere in its 249 pages is John Morrissey mentioned. As they had in his own lifetime, for most of the twentieth century Morrissey's vast and varied contributions to American sports went almost entirely unrecognized. The Saratoga Race Course had fallen onto hard times in the 1890s, run nearly into the ground by a shady gambler, racetrack operator, and brothel keeper named Gottfried "Dutch Fred" Waldbaum. A group headed by William Collins Whitney, a wealthy patrician and former secretary of the navy, purchased the track from Waldbaum, and the new owners were rightly praised by horsemen and journalists for restoring Saratoga to its former glory. Following his death in 1904 Whitney was embraced as a "founding father" of Saratoga in an era in which Thoroughbred racing was beset by "progressive" reformers determined to rid the nation of horse racing once and for all. In that environment, even the memory of John Morrissey was a liability for the sport.

Morrissey received a modicum of recognition in 1996, when he was inducted into the International Boxing Hall of Fame, joining the likes of Joe Louis, Muhammad Ali, and Jack Dempsey in enshrinement. Morrissey's legend is also kept alive through the historical tours given in Saratoga Springs at the building that once housed America's most vibrant and lavish casino. In 1881 Susie Morrissey was at Saratoga Race Course to witness the John Morrissey Stakes, which would be run at various distances through the end of the nineteenth century before being put on a hundred-year hiatus early in the twentieth. The revived John Morrissey Stakes, a middling sprint race restricted to New York–bred horses, is now an annual fixture at Saratoga. Although his namesake pales in prestige to races such as the Travers Stakes and the Whitney and Vanderbilt Handicaps, John Morrissey did more than anyone else in furtherance of horse racing at Saratoga. His legacy endures at America's oldest major sports venue, where, a century and a half after its founding, thousands of racing enthusiasts gather each summer in celebration of the sporting life promoted and embodied by its chief architect.

Acknowledgments

There were various stages at which I did not believe this book would see the light of day. Therefore, I am especially grateful to the many people who helped this project come to fruition.

Agnes Hamberger at the Saratoga Springs History Museum shared her enthusiasm for the history of her town with me. David Null gave me access to the Fred Harvey Harrington papers at the University of Wisconsin–Madison Archives. The staffs at the New York Public Library Schwarzman Building Periodicals and Microform Room, Saratoga Springs Public Library, Troy New York Public Library, and Rensselaer County Historical Society were all helpful and accommodating. The Keeneland Library and William T. Young Library at the University of Kentucky were welcoming as ever.

Words of support and kind gestures from Alex Bushel, Quin Bell, Will Coffman, Libby Jones, Patrick Lewis, Laura and Zack Bray, Walt Robertson, Barrett Milner, David and Jamay Shook, Matt Halloran, Richard Mandella, Alex Lieblong, Helen Alexander, Benny and John Williams, Gary Mandella, Gemma Freeman, Nancy Bell, and Corky Robertson were much appreciated.

My introduction to Saratoga came years ago as a member of the Fasig-Tipton stable crew. My time there performing tasks that included loading large burlap sacks filled with horse manure onto a trailer included plenty of early morning laughs with Austin Groves, Drew Wooldridge, Woody Moore, Mark "Snake" Thompson, Chris Elser, Russell Lencki, Al Plan, Daren English, Ralph Petruzzo, and others.

151

Acknowledgments

Maryjean Wall, Ed Bowen, and an anonymous reviewer provided helpful feedback on an early draft of this book, and Liz Smith's careful copyediting greatly enhanced the manuscript. Everyone at the University Press of Kentucky, including Anne Dean Dotson, David Cobb, Amy Harris, Patrick O'Dowd, Bailey Johnson, Cameron Ludwick, Mack McCormick, and Pat Gonzales, has been friendly and professional as always.

Notes

Introduction

1. *New York Times,* May 5, 1878, 7.
2. "A Dead Lion," *Puck,* May 8, 1878, 2.

1. Wharf Rat

1. "Death of John Morrissey," *New York Times,* May 2, 1878, 1; "Senator Morrissey Dead," *New York Sun,* May 2, 1878. Morrissey's obituary in the *Sun* states that the family lived briefly in Quebec before moving to Troy. Most other sources imply that the family entered the United States in New York City. The specific reference to Quebec in the *Sun* lends credence to that assertion, though the *Sun*'s claim that the family left Ireland when John was five years old puts that date two years later than other accounts. The family settled first in West Troy before moving across the river.
2. "Death of John Morrissey," *New York Times,* May 2, 1878, 1.
3. "A Card from John Morrissey," *Natchez Daily Courier,* Nov. 29, 1866; *San Francisco Daily Evening Bulletin,* Dec. 6, 1866; *New York Tribune,* Nov. 3, 1877; *New York Sun,* May 2, 1878. Hamilton's full first name was Alexander, but he is not to be confused with the American founding father of the same name.
4. "John Morrissey at Home," *Chicago Daily Tribune,* Aug. 8, 1874, 4.
5. "Death of John Morrissey," *New York Times,* May 2, 1878, 1.
6. "Senator Morrissey Dead," *New York Sun,* May 2, 1878. Another version of this story has Morrissey's future father-in-law, Captain Levi Smith, making the claims of Morrissey's prowess to Dutch Charley. See Edward Hotaling, *They're Off! Horse Racing at Saratoga* (Syracuse, N.Y.: Syracuse University Press, 1995), 30.

153

7. "The Great Prize Fight between Tom Hyer and Yankee Sullivan for Ten Thousand Dollars," *Spirit of the Times,* Feb. 17, 1849. The anticipation for the match had "engaged thousands of minds for a period of six long months." McCleester seems to have answered to a number of names, including McCloskey, McClusky, and McCheester.

8. The fight originally had been scheduled for Poole's Island in the Chesapeake Bay, but a police raid forced fight organizers to remove it to Still Pond Heights in Kent County at the mouth of the Gunpowder River.

9. George Gipe, "Run, Sullivan! Run!," *Sports Illustrated,* Sept. 30, 1974.

10. *Stroudsburg (Pa.) Jeffersonian Republican,* Feb. 15, 1849; *Sunbury (Pa.) American,* Feb. 17, 1849.

11. For a good description of the Sullivan-Hyer fight, see Elliott J. Gorn, *The Manly Art: Bare-Knuckle Prize Fighting in America* (Ithaca, N.Y.: Cornell University Press, 1986), 85–96.

12. "Senator Morrissey Dead," *New York Sun,* May 2, 1878; "John Morrissey at Home," *Chicago Daily Tribune,* Aug. 1, 1874, 4.

13. *San Francisco Daily Evening Bulletin,* Jun. 16, 1884.

14. See Tyler Anbinder, *Five Points: The 19th-Century New York City Neighborhood That Invented Tap Dance, Stole Elections, and Became the World's Most Notorious Slum* (New York: Plume, 2002), 141; "Isaiah Rynders, Captain of the Empire Club, New York City," *New York Herald,* Feb. 2, 1845; Sherlock Bristol, *Pioneer Preacher,* 666–67, quoted in Anbinder, *Five Points; New York Times,* Jan. 14, 1885.

15. See "Praise of Capt. Rynders," *New York Times,* Jan. 14, 1885.

16. "Isaiah Rynders, Captain of the Empire Club, New York City," *New York Herald,* Feb. 2, 1845; Nigel Cliff, *The Shakespeare Riots: Revenge, Drama, and Death in Nineteenth-Century New York* (New York: Random House, 2007), 196. Rynders would later claim credit for helping to facilitate the election of Presidents Franklin Pierce and James Buchanan, the latter of whom rewarded Rynders with an appointment as a U.S. marshal.

17. *Church Monthly,* Mar. 1858, quoted in Anbinder, *Five Points,* 1. In May 1849 Rynders was a major instigator of the Astor Place Riot, which left some twenty-five dead and well over one hundred injured. The bloody disturbance grew out of an ethnically charged dispute

over which of the two leading Shakespearean actors of the day—one an American, the other British—was the world's top thespian. Rynders found support for the American among the Irish gangs of the Five Points and worked to foment civic unrest that resulted in state militia firing live rounds into the riotous mob.

18. "John Morrissey at Home," *Chicago Daily Tribune,* Aug. 1, 1874, 4; "Senator Morrissey Dead," *New York Sun,* May 2, 1878.

19. John Eisenberg, *The Great Match Race: When North Met South in America's First Sports Spectacle* (Boston: Houghton Mifflin, 2006), describes the first of these match races.

20. See Jackson Lears's broader discussion of "the constantly shifting tensions between rivalrous American cultures of chance and control" and "the face-off between the confidence man, the devotee of Fortuna, and the self-made man, the herald of Providence," in *Something for Nothing: Luck in America* (New York: Viking, 2003), 4.

21. The *New York Daily Tribune,* May 14, 1845, called the crowd "a larger collection of people than we have ever before seen at the Union Course."

22. "John Morrissey at Home," *Chicago Daily Tribune,* Aug. 1, 1874, 4. The *New York Sun,* May 2, 1878, places Morrissey's fateful visit to New York City in the fall of 1848 rather than in 1849, which is implied in the *Tribune* interview.

23. "John Morrissey at Home," *Chicago Tribune,* Aug. 1, 1874, 4 (quotes); "Senator Morrissey Dead," *New York Sun,* May 2, 1878.

24. Some versions, including that recounted in Morrissey's obituary in the *New York Sun,* place the fight in Sandy Lawrence's pistol gallery beneath the St. Charles Hotel at Broadway and Leonard Street. Other sources identify the hotel as the St. James.

25. See, for example, William E. Harding, *John Morrissey, His Life, Battles, and Wrangles, from His Birth in Ireland until He Died a State Senator* (New York, 1881).

26. "John Morrissey at Home," *Chicago Daily Tribune,* Aug. 1, 1874, 4.

27. The *New York Times* places the year of his departure for California at 1850 in "Death of John Morrissey," May 2, 1878, 1; others, including *New York Sun,* May 2, 1878, claim it was 1851. It is possible that he departed in 1850 and arrived in 1851. The *Times* article also claimed that he stowed away on a Pacific Mail steamer in New

York. The Pacific Mail operated between New York and Chagres from 1850 until April 1851, when the company sold its Atlantic fleet to the U.S. Mail Steamship Company. When asked years later in a criminal trial about his occupation, Dad, who stood five feet four inches tall and weighed one hundred pounds, declined to answer the question, offering only, "I don't steal or rob." *New York Daily Times,* Mar. 13, 1855, 1.

28. See "A Journey from New York to San Francisco," *American Historical Review* 9, no. 1 (Oct. 1903), 104–15.

29. "Death of John Morrissey," *New York Times,* May 2, 1878, 1. According to the *Times,* the boys stowed away on the *Panama,* a Pacific Mail ship bound for San Francisco. That article also claims that a Captain Hudson was in charge of the vessel. The online database of the Maritime Heritage Project containing San Francisco ship records for that era shows a Captain Hudson on the *Panama,* but not until 1853. Captain Hudson did work the route from Panama to San Francisco on the SS *Republic* on a regular basis from 1850 to 1852.

30. "Death of John Morrissey," *New York Times,* May 2, 1878, 1. The Queen Charlotte Islands are now officially known as Haida Gwaii.

31. "Death of John Morrissey," *New York Times,* May 2, 1878, 1.

32. See Gorn, *The Manly Art,* 81–95. In the lead-up to the much-publicized Hyer-Sullivan fight, American journalists ignored Hyer's significant connections to the New York gangland underworld and portrayed him as a hardworking butcher and a model citizen of the American working class as contrasted with Sullivan, whom they described as an example of unskilled Irish labor—a process that would be repeated in the lead-up to Morrissey's final fight, with John C. Heenan. According to Herbert Asbury, *Sucker's Progress: An Informal History of Gambling in America* (1938; New York: Thunder's Mouth, 2003), 371, the stakes were $2,000 per side plus a $1,000 side bet.

33. See Peter Gammie, "Pugilists and Politicians in Antebellum New York: The Life and Times of Tom Hyer," *New York History* 75, no. 3 (Jul. 1994): 265.

34. Mare Island was named after an incident in which a prized white mare belonging to Mexican general Mariano Guadalupe Vallejo was lost when a transport ship capsized in the area. The mare was found on what had formerly been called Isla de la Plana.

35. "Great Prize Fight in California: Morrissey vs. Thompson," *Spirit of the Times,* Oct. 9, 1852.

36. Gary F. Kurutz, "Popular Culture on the Golden Shore," in *Rooted in Barbarous Soil: People, Culture, and Community in Gold Rush California,* ed. Kevin Starr and Richard J. Orsi (Berkeley: University of California Press, 2000), 303. The fans from Sacramento "bet houses and lots very freely against horses and other livestock."

37. *St. Louis Globe-Democrat,* Aug. 31, 1880, 3. Other sources claimed that the stakes were $2,500 per side.

38. Gorn, *The Manly Art,* 75.

39. "Great Prize Fight in California: Morrissey vs. Thompson," *Spirit of the Times,* Oct. 9, 1852.

40. "Great Prize Fight in California: Morrissey vs. Thompson," *Spirit of the Times,* Oct. 9, 1852.

41. See Gorn, *The Manly Art,* 110. Morrissey's *New York Times* obituary ("Death of John Morrissey," May 2, 1878) says the fight lasted nineteen minutes. Other sources say it was sixteen minutes. The *National Police Gazette,* Jul. 3, 1880, perpetuated the rumors of untoward doings at the fight on Mare Island: "After 11 desperate-fought rounds, of which six were knock-downs for Thompson, Morrissey was declared the winner by a foul blow which Thompson purposely struck to lose the fight, being afraid of being shot. The fight lasted 16 minutes, and Morrissey received the lion's share of the punishment."

42. See Kurutz, "Popular Culture on the Golden Shore," 303.

43. According to Hotaling, *They're Off!,* 31, Morrissey and his friends were able to pay for their trip home to New York with proceeds from a sizable bet on a black mare named Carmencita in a ten-mile match race against the bay mare Alameda in Santa Barbara.

44. *Barre (Mass.) Patriot,* Oct. 28, 1853.

2. Fighter

1. "New York City: Sporting Intelligence," *New York Times,* Jul. 29, 1854.

2. "John Morrissey at Home," *Chicago Daily Tribune,* Aug. 1, 1874, 4; *National Police Gazette,* Jul. 3, 1880; Peter Gammie, "Pugilists and Politicians in Antebellum New York: The Life and Times of Tom Hyer," *New York History* 75, no. 3 (Jul. 1994): 287. His *New York Times* obituary ("Death of John Morrissey," May 2, 1878) says the forfeit was $250.

3. "Yankee Sullivan No More," *New York Daily Times,* Jun. 30, 1856, 1; Elliott J. Gorn, *The Manly Art: Bare-Knuckle Prize Fighting in America* (Ithaca, N.Y.: Cornell University Press, 1986), 69–70. In addition to James Ambrose, the name probably given to him at birth, Sullivan had earlier gone by the names Frank Murray, Francis Murray, and Francis Martin.

4. "The $2,000 Fight: Yankee Sullivan vs. John Morrissey," *New York Daily Times,* Oct. 13, 1853, 1.

5. *Washington Daily Evening Star,* Oct. 14, 1853, citing the *New York Herald.* Journalistic descriptions of the fight vary significantly. This is perhaps due to different political allegiances of the papers and the probability that some of the writers were reporting secondhand information.

6. "The Late Prize Fight: Sullivan vs. Morrissey," *Spirit of the Times,* Oct. 22, 1853, 421; *Washington Daily Evening Star,* Oct. 14, 1853, citing the *New York Herald.*

7. "John Morrissey's Fight with Yankee Sullivan," *San Francisco Call,* May 8, 1910; "The Late Prize Fight: Sullivan vs. Morrissey," *Spirit of the Times,* Oct. 22, 1853, 421.

8. "The Late Prize Fight: Sullivan vs. Morrissey," *Spirit of the Times,* Oct. 22, 1853, 421.

9. *Washington Daily Evening Star,* Oct. 14, 1853, citing the *New York Herald;* "The Late Prize Fight: Sullivan vs. Morrissey," *Spirit of the Times,* Oct. 22, 1853, 421. Awful Gardner's brother was named Howell "Horrible" Gardner. Gardner had a distinguished fighting career in New Jersey before legal trouble forced him to abscond to New York City, where he met John Morrissey when both men were working as immigrant runners. Both Awful and Horrible Gardner later became Christian ministers.

10. See Gorn, *The Manly Art,* 110–11.

11. *New York Times,* May 2, 1878, 1.

12. "John Morrissey at Home," *Chicago Daily Tribune,* Aug. 1, 1874, 4.

13. "The Late Prize Fight: Sullivan vs. Morrissey," *Spirit of the Times,* Oct. 22, 1853, 421.

14. *New York Daily Times,* Oct. 15, 1853; *Daily Cleveland (Ohio) Herald,* Oct. 14, 1853. Morrissey was reported as having died in the bout by the *Fayetteville (N.C.) Observer,* Oct. 23, 1853.

15. "The Prize Fight between Sullivan and Morrissey," *New York Times,* Oct. 14, 1853.

16. See Gorn, *The Manly Art,* 111; *New York Times,* Nov. 8, 1853; Arthur Myers, "The Brawls at Boston Corners," *Sports Illustrated,* Apr. 2, 1973.

17. "The Late Prize Fight: Sullivan vs. Morrissey," *Spirit of the Times,* Oct. 22, 1853, 421.

18. *New York Daily Times,* Jul. 28, 1854, 4. The *New York Sun,* May 2, 1878, places the encounter at Dick Platt's saloon under Wallack's Theater. Morrissey had a history with Hughes, including a run-in on the steamboat from New York to Panama.

19. *National Police Gazette,* Sept. 18, 1880, 4. According to a different account of the evening's events, Poole's patrons threw a ball for him at the Chinese Assembly Room. People came from as far away as Savannah, Charleston, and New Orleans. Morrissey was in attendance but left at 10:00 p.m. and walked down to the City Hotel for a drink. Poole came by later and found Morrissey smoking a cigar. Morrissey said, "Here comes the black-muzzled American fighter." Poole replied, "Yes, and I'm a dandy." Morrissey then issued a challenge. "Yes, you are a dandy, and I can lick you tomorrow morning," he said. "And what's more, I will bet you $500 that you dare not meet me and fight me. You can name the place of the meeting." *National Police Gazette,* Sept. 11, 1880, 14.

20. *New York Weekly Herald,* Jul. 29, 1854; W. E. Harding, "The American Prize-Ring," *National Police Gazette,* Sept. 18, 1880, 4; *New York Times,* Jul. 28, 1854. The *New York Tribune* reported that both men arrived by wagon.

21. *New York Daily Times,* Jul. 28, 1854. Another group of supporters made it only as far as a nearby saloon, where one Poole partisan, "Smut" Ackerman, died as a result of a head injury sustained while trying to demonstrate Poole's takedown of Morrissey.

22. *New York Times,* Jul. 29, 1854. One witness claimed that there was no crowd interference and that "not a hand was raised to interfere with or favor either contestant. If Morrissey ever had a square deal, he had it" at the Poole fight, and the crowd only became involved in the attack on Morrissey after the fight had concluded. It was then that, in the racist parlance of the times, the large gang of Poole supporters turned on the "sports and outsiders" in the crowd and "went for them like an

alligator for a plump pickaninny and ornamented their countenances in various eccentric ways, simply to keep their joints from stiffening." See The[odore] Allen, "The True Story of the Poole-Morrissey Fight," *National Police Gazette*, Sept. 18, 1880.

23. *Pittsfield (Mass.) Sun*, Aug. 3, 1854.

24. "Statement of Morrissey," *New York Times*, Jul. 29, 1854.

25. *Troy Times*, Aug. 11, 1854.

26. "John Morrissey at Home," *Chicago Daily Tribune*, Aug. 1, 1874, 4; *Maine Farmer*, Aug. 31, 1872, 3.

27. Elliott J. Gorn, "'Good-Bye Boys, I Die a True American': Homicide, Nativism, and Working-Class Culture in Antebellum New York City," *Journal of American History* 74, no. 2 (Sept. 1987): 393–94.

28. M. R. Werner, *Tammany Hall* (Garden City, N.J.: Doubleday, Doran and Company, 1928), 74. See also Jerome Mushkat, *Fernando Wood: A Political Biography* (Kent, Ohio: Kent State University Press, 1990), 34–36.

29. *New York Morning Courier and Enquirer*, Nov. 9, 1854, quoted in Werner, *Tammany Hall*, 78.

30. See Samuel Augustus Pleasants, *Fernando Wood of New York* (New York: Columbia University Press, 1948), 11–18, 24–32.

31. Herbert Asbury, *Sucker's Progress: An Informal History of Gambling in America* (1938; New York: Thunder's Mouth, 2003), 372–76.

32. "John Morrissey's Teacher," *The Youth's Companion*, Dec. 25, 1879.

33. "John Morrissey at Home," *Chicago Daily Tribune*, Aug. 1, 1874, 4.

34. "Rearrest of Morrissey," *New York Times*, Sept. 15, 1854; "The Poole Murder," *New York Daily Times*, Mar. 15, 1855, 3; *New York Daily Times*, Mar. 13, 1855, 1. The descriptions of the events of the night of February 24, 1855, in the coroner's inquest and trial transcripts were widely reported in the various New York newspapers. They were often contradictory, but a general narrative emerges from a composite of the varied testimony.

35. "The Poole Murder," *New York Daily Times*, Mar. 15, 1855, 3; *New York Daily Times*, Mar. 9, 1855; *New York Daily Times*, Mar. 13, 1855, 1; Gorn, "'Good-Bye Boys, I Die a True American,'" 389. Some witnesses claimed that Poole had climbed on top of the bar dur-

ing an anti-Irish rant. Others swear that he was never on the bar and that he may not even have been armed.

36. "The Poole Murder," *New York Daily Times*, Mar. 15, 1855, 3.

37. "The Poole Murder," *New York Daily Times*, Mar. 13, 1855, 1; *New York Daily Times*, Mar. 15, 1855, 3; *New York Daily Times*, Dec. 8, 1855. A barkeeper at Stanwix Hall testified that Morrissey's long trip home even included a return visit to the Stanwix before he and Dad left together around 12:30 a.m. See *New York Daily Times*, Mar. 19, 1855.

38. *New York Daily Times*, Feb. 26, 1855; Gorn, "'Good-Bye Boys, I Die a True American,'" 390.

39. "The Pugilists' Encounter," *New York Daily Times*, Mar. 9, 1855.

40. *New York Daily Times*, Mar. 12, 1855, 1; Gorn, "'Good-Bye Boys, I Die a True American,'" 391.

41. *Brooklyn Eagle*, Mar. 20, 1855.

42. *New York Tribune*, Mar. 19, 1855.

43. *New York Tribune*, Mar. 15, 1855. According to the *New York Times*, Nov. 28, 1855, Isaiah Rynders was seated at Baker's counsel's table during the trial.

44. *New York Observer and Chronicle*, Apr. 26, 1855; *Maine Farmer*, Apr. 24, 1856, 2.

45. See "Murder Trials: The Poole Tragedy," *New York Daily Times*, Apr. 19, 1855; *New York Observer and Chronicle*, Apr. 26, 1855.

46. Throughout his life, Morrissey treated women and children with particular compassion, a tendency that was on display during a train ride from New York to Buffalo the year of his son's birth. Two men, who had clearly been drinking, entered the car where Morrissey was seated. They were talking loudly and telling crude stories in front of two women and a small child. Morrissey sympathized with the ladies, who were visibly uncomfortable in the presence of the obnoxious fellows, and said, "Come, boys, let's go into the smoking car and have a good cigar." When the men declined, Morrissey took a seat in front of them and asked them to lower their voices. The men ignored the request and resumed their loud banter. After a repeated request yielded an instruction from the two men to mind his own business, Morrissey

responded, "My business is to protect ladies from insult, and if either of you says another improper word I will pitch you both out of the car." The men stood to confront Morrissey, who grabbed their heads and knocked them together. He asked the conductor to open the car door so that he could drag one and push the other into the smoking car. "The Sort of Man Morrissey Is," *Saturday Evening Post*, Nov. 17, 1877, 367.

47. Mushkat, *Fernando Wood*, 58–59.

48. *New York Daily Tribune*, May 7, 1857; "Desperate Fight at the Girard House," *New York Times*, May 7, 1857; Denis Tilden Lynch, *"Boss" Tweed: The Story of a Grim Generation* (New Brunswick, N.J.: Transaction, 2002), 120.

49. *New York Daily Times*, May 8, 1857, 4; *New York Sun*, May 2, 1878 (quote). Petrie was also jailed as a result of the incident. After initially making bail, Morrissey was rearrested a week later on additional charges filed by the police officers who had tried to arrest him. See *New York Daily Times*, May 13, 1857, 2; *New York Daily Times*, Dec. 25, 1855, 3; *New York Herald*, Jul. 30, 1856; *New York Times*, May 7, 1857; Gammie, "Pugilists and Politicians in Antebellum New York," 265.

50. J. T. Headley, *The Great Riots of New York, 1712 to 1873* (New York: E. B. Treat, 1873), 131–32.

51. See Fred H. Harrington, untitled biography of John Morrissey, Fred H. Harrington Papers, University of Wisconsin–Madison Archives, Box 16.

52. *New York Daily Times*, Mar. 22, 1858, 4, 8; *New York Times*, Mar. 24, 1858; *New York Times*, Mar. 25, 1858, 5.

53. *New York Daily Times*, Mar. 23, 1858. Morrissey, who was spending more time in Troy, operating the Ivy Green saloon there, visited Cunningham in jail. While the public attention paid to McLaughlin's death paled in comparison to that surrounding the Bill Poole memorial, a column sympathetic to the fallen gangster appearing in the *New York Herald* caused the *New York Times* to complain that "the greatest poet, orator, scholar, soldier or patriot of our day would certainly not have as much space devoted to the dismal record of his last agonies as 'Paudeen' enjoys in the columns of [the *Herald*]." *New York Daily Times*, Mar. 25, 1858, 4.

54. Gorn, *The Manly Art*, 113–14.

3. Champion

1. Elliott J. Gorn, *The Manly Art: Bare-Knuckle Prize Fighting in America* (Ithaca, N.Y.: Cornell University Press, 1986), 115–16.

2. "John Morrissey at Home," *Chicago Daily Tribune,* Aug. 1, 1874, 4.

3. Gorn, *The Manly Art,* 116.

4. "John Morrissey a 'Lion,'" *New York Times,* Sept. 1, 1858, 2; *New York Clipper,* Oct. 30, 1858; Edward Hotaling, *They're Off! Horse Racing at Saratoga* (Syracuse, N.Y.: Syracuse University Press, 1995), 35.

5. *New York Clipper,* Oct. 30, 1858.

6. *New York Tribune,* Oct. 20, 1858; "The Fight for the Championship," *Frank Leslie's Illustrated Newspaper,* Oct. 30, 1858, 344.

7. "The Fight for the Championship: Particulars of the Great Mill between Morrissey and Heenan," *New York Times,* Oct. 22, 1858, 5.

8. "The Fight for the Championship: Particulars of the Great Mill between Morrissey and Heenan," *New York Times,* Oct. 22, 1858, 5; Gorn, *The Manly Art,* 118.

9. *New York Tribune,* Oct. 22, 1858, quoted in Dennis Gildea, "'Cross-Counter': The Heenan-Morrissey Fight of 1858 and Frank Queen's Attack on the "'Respectable Press,'" *Colby Quarterly* 32, no. 1 (1996): 11–22.

10. *New York Sun,* May 2, 1878; "The Fight for the Championship," *Frank Leslie's Illustrated Newspaper,* Oct. 30, 1858, 344. Even the rowboats could get to within only thirty or forty feet of land because of sandbars, so patrons wound up wading the rest of the way or paying crewmen to carry them to shore on their shoulders.

11. William E. Harding, "The American Prize-Ring," *National Police Gazette,* Oct. 23, 1880, 15; Gorn, *The Manly Art,* 118.

12. "The Coming Prize Fight," *New York Times,* Oct. 18, 1855.

13. "The Great Prize Fight," *Spirit of the Times,* Oct. 30, 1858, 449. The *New York Times* claimed that Heenan hurt his knuckles in round four. "The Fight for the Championship: Particulars of the Great Mill between Morrissey and Heenan," *New York Times,* Oct. 22, 1858.

14. "Championship of the Prize Ring—The Great Fight between Morrissey and Heenan," *Milwaukee Daily Sentinel,* Oct. 26, 1858; *New York Times,* Oct. 22, 1858, 5; "The Great Prize Fight," *Spirit of the Times,* Oct. 30, 1858, 449; William E. Harding, "The American Prize-Ring," *National Police Gazette,* Oct. 23, 1880, 15.

15. "Championship of the Prize Ring—The Great Fight between Morrissey and Heenan," *Milwaukee Daily Sentinel,* Oct. 26, 1858.

16. "The Great Prize Fight," *Spirit of the Times,* Oct. 30, 1858, 449 (quote); William E. Harding, "The American Prize-Ring," *National Police Gazette,* Oct. 23, 1880, 15.

17. "The Great Prize Fight," *Spirit of the Times,* Oct. 30, 1858, 449.

18. "John Morrissey at Home," *Chicago Daily Tribune,* Aug. 1, 1874, 4.

19. *New York Tribune,* Oct. 22, 1858; "The Fight for the Championship," *Frank Leslie's Illustrated Newspaper,* Oct. 30, 1858. See also Gorn, *The Manly Art,* 120.

20. "The Fight for the Championship: Particulars of the Great Mill between Morrissey and Heenan," *New York Times,* Oct. 22, 1858.

21. *New York Tribune,* Oct. 22, 1858.

22. See, for example, *National Era,* Nov. 18, 1858.

23. *New York Times,* Oct. 30, 1858, 8. Heenan would soon find his name in newspaper headlines for his scandalous affair and marriage to actress Adah Isaacs Mencken. See John Dizikes, *Sportsmen and Gentlemen: From the Years That Shaped American Ideas about Winning and Losing and How to Play the Game* (Boston: Houghton Mifflin, 1981), 193–236.

24. *New Orleans Crescent,* Jan. 10, 1869, citing the *New York Mercury.* See also Edwin G. Burrows and Mike Wallace, *Gotham: A History of New York City to 1898* (New York: Oxford University Press, 1999), 955; Henry Chafetz, *Play the Devil: A History of Gambling in the United States from 1492 to 1955* (1960; rpt., London: Forgotten Books, 2013), 281–82.

25. *New York Evangelist,* Mar. 22, 1860, 4.

26. "John Morrissey at Home," *Chicago Daily Tribune,* Aug. 1, 1874, 4.

27. *Jackson (Miss.) Daily News,* May 15, 1860.

28. Samuel Augustus Pleasants, *Fernando Wood of New York* (New York: Columbia University Press, 1948), 114–15.

4. Saratoga

1. George Waller, *Saratoga: Saga of an Impious Era* (New York: Bonanza Books, 1966), 3–9. Other sources claim that the springs John-

son visited were not the Saratoga springs and that his visit came in 1767. But the real significance of the story lies in the fact that the visit became part of the legend and identity of Saratoga. The name Saratoga traces back to a seventeenth-century Dutch fort, which borrowed an Indian name for the area that surrounded the upper Hudson River. See also Thomas A. Chambers, *Drinking the Waters: Creating an American Leisure Class at Nineteenth-Century Mineral Springs* (Washington, D.C.: Smithsonian Institution Press, 2002), 33. Morrissey was operating as a gambler in Saratoga at least as early as 1860, but he opened his own establishment in 1861. See, for example, "Personal," *New York Times,* Aug. 25, 1860.

2. Waller, *Saratoga,* 58.

3. Waller, *Saratoga,* 59; Chambers, *Drinking the Waters,* 26. Putnam's Boarding House would continue to be expanded over the years. It would be renamed Union Hall and, later, the Grand Union Hotel, which eventually would lay claim to being the largest hotel in the world.

4. See Waller, *Saratoga,* 66–70; Chambers, *Drinking the Waters,* 28–33, 52.

5. Chambers, *Drinking the Waters,* 13. The railroad increased the number of annual visitors to Saratoga Springs to eight thousand.

6. Waller, *Saratoga,* 76. See also Nathaniel Bartlett Sylvester, *History of Saratoga County, New York* (Philadelphia: Everts and Ensign, 1878). Davison was a newspaper publisher who also published early tourist guidebooks, further encouraging the growing tourist industry in upstate New York.

7. Waller, *Saratoga,* 79.

8. Philip Hone, "August 12, 1839," *The Diaries of Philip Hone,* vol. 1 (Ithaca, N.Y.: Cornell University Library, 2014), 376. Despite the diverse crowd, the excitement level during the day at Saratoga was rather low. For many the most exhilarating activity was a ride to Saratoga Lake a few miles outside of town. The lake was for some years merely a nominal destination—a "vacation from the vacation." But eventually lakefront restaurants were established, including Moon's Lake House, which, according to an inaccurate but persistent legend, became the birthplace of potato chips when an unhappy customer continued to complain about his fried potatoes being too thick. A frustrated chef supposedly sliced the potatoes razor thin and fried them to a crisp. To the chef's surprise, the customer loved them. An authorized

biography of the chef, a mixed-race Native American hunting guide, made no claim to the invention, and there is no evidence to support the oft-repeated tale. Recipes for thinly sliced potatoes appeared in print as early as the 1820s. In later versions of the story, Commodore Cornelius Vanderbilt was the customer who ordered his potatoes to be cut more thinly.

9. *New York Times,* Jun. 26, 1866, 5; *Indianapolis State Sentinel,* Aug. 30, 1865, citing the *Troy Times; Wheeling Daily Intelligencer,* Jul. 27, 1866.

10. By the summer of 1863 the war was finally turning in the Union's favor. But in the early stages, President Abraham Lincoln had been frustrated by his officers' deliberate tendencies. According to one tale, Lincoln told Secretary of War Edwin Stanton that his generals' habit of telegraphing the War Department at every opportunity, and at the expense of more decisive action, reminded him of a story involving John Morrissey in which a Morrissey henchman told a compatriot of his plans to get married. The man issued congratulations but then asked, "Did ye ask Morrissey yet?" Regardless of its veracity, the story serves as an indication of Morrissey's rising stature in American popular culture. See Carleton B. Case, *Humor of Abraham Lincoln, Gathered from Authentic Sources* (Chicago: Shrewesbury, 1916), 98–99. According to legend, Morrissey and his wife were introduced to Lincoln at a ball held in New York City honoring the president-elect. See Jon Bartles, *Saratoga Stories: Gangsters, Gamblers, and Racing Legends* (Lexington, Ky.: Eclipse, 2007), 27.

11. *Washington Daily National Republican,* Jul. 22, 1863. Edward Hotaling, *They're Off! Horse Racing at Saratoga* (Syracuse, N.Y.: Syracuse University Press, 1995), 41, claims that Morrissey was dining in his New York City saloon during the riots in New York City, but he cites a notoriously unreliable source. Later that summer, when Morrissey himself was drafted, the announcement in New York City "drew forth several cheers." He paid the $300 commutation fee and avoided service. A story later circulated in various American papers that Morrissey was offering $5,000 for a soldier willing to take his place in the army. That gaudy sum was far in excess of the statutory $300 service-avoidance fee, so the veracity of the story was suspect at best, but outrage filled editorial pages around the nation. See "The Draft," *New York Times,* Aug. 21, 1863; "Exemption Claims," *New York Times,*

Aug. 28, 1863; "A Princely Pugilist," *Clearfield (Pa.) Republican,* Sept. 9, 1863.

12. *Daily Saratogian,* Jul. 27–31, 1863, 2, quoted in Hotaling, *They're Off!,* 42–43. The published announcement was signed by "John Morrissey, Proprietor." The *Washington Daily National Republican* reported on May 26, 1863, "John Morrissey has leased the race track at Saratoga for the summer season. A number of races are already announced to come off."

13. *Saratoga Republican,* Aug. 4, 1863, quoted in Landon Manning, *The Noble Animals: Tales of the Saratoga Turf* (Saratoga, N.Y.: Landon Manning, 1973), 64.

14. Some twentieth-century historians have concluded that the immensely popular Lady Suffolk was the inspiration for the song "The Old Gray Mare (She Ain't What She Used to Be)," and some credit Stephen C. Foster with writing it. But there is no conclusive evidence that Foster wrote the song or that it was written about Lady Suffolk, whose victory in that early Saratoga event was a series of one-mile heats for a purse of $150. To skirt the gambling prohibition, the organizers of those early trotting races at Saratoga called their event "trials of speed," to be given as an "exhibition" in conjunction with the state fair (even though the meet got under way weeks before the fair came to town). The *Spirit of the Times,* Aug. 21, 1847, reported: "The attendance was very large, and the road to the track was crowded with pedestrians, equestrians, and carriages of all kinds. About five thousand persons were present; among the spectators were a number of lovely women from the South, whose interest in the event seemed greater even than that of the gentlemen." Later in the meet, the first organized Thoroughbred running race in Saratoga was won by Lady Digby.

15. See Manning, *The Noble Animals,* citing *Wilkes' Spirit of the Times;* John Eisenberg, *The Great Match Race: When North Met South in America's First Sports Spectacle* (Boston: Houghton Mifflin, 2006), 238–39. Some contemporary accounts say that there was no grandstand left from the original trotting meet, and others say that it was still there but rotten.

16. "The Saratoga Running Races," *New York Times,* Jul. 29, 1863, 8.

17. "Robert H. Underwood," *New York Times,* Dec. 15, 1874. A writer in the sporting journal *Horseman* described Underwood as "a

Jew" with "the magnetism of the Israelites to draw the scrip out of the pockets of the 'innocents abroad' who were anxious to get rich quick on other people's money," according to Steven A. Riess, *The Sport of Kings and the Kings of Crime: Horse Racing, Politics, and Organized Crime in New York, 1865–1913* (Syracuse, N.Y.: Syracuse University Press, 2011), 16, citing Bernard Postal, Jesse Silver, and Roy Silver, *Encyclopedia of Jews in Sports* (New York: Bloch, 1965), 329.

18. See Hotaling, *They're Off!,* 46; Katherine C. Mooney, *Race Horse Men: How Slavery and Freedom Were Made at the Racetrack* (Cambridge, Mass.: Harvard University Press, 2014), 138. Eight horses were originally entered, but by post time six had been withdrawn, leaving Captain Moore, among the top three-year-old colts of the year and ridden by Billy Burgoyne, as Lizzy W.'s only rival.

19. Gilpatrick's obituary, *New York Times,* Nov. 25, 1882, states that the great jockey rode in five thousand races "and was a winner in four-fifths of these" (a dubious claim, though one that would be difficult to authoritatively disprove). The obituarist lamented that although Gilpatrick had "won over $2,000,000 in stakes in the races in which he rode for the gentlemen whose horses he mounted," he was "in absolute want of the necessities of life at the time of his death. To their discredit be it said that when appealed to for assistance, the gentlemen for whom he had won thousands of dollars absolutely refused assistance." Morrissey's colt was originally named Jerome Edger, but he renamed him. Some sources list Thunder's name as Thunderer.

20. *Saratoga Republican,* Aug. 4, 1863, quoted in Manning, *The Noble Animals,* 64.

21. *Saratoga Republican,* Aug. 4, 1863, quoted in Manning, *The Noble Animals,* 64.

22. *New York Times,* Aug. 5, 1863, 5; *New York Times,* Aug. 7, 1863, 5. After a quick thundershower, the horse Captain Moore returned for his second race of the week and captured three straight one-mile heats.

23. *Wilkes' Spirit of the Times,* quoted in Manning, *The Noble Animals,* 64.

24. "John Morrissey at Home," *Chicago Daily Tribune,* Aug. 1, 1874, 4.

25. See T. J. Stiles, *The First Tycoon: The Epic Life of Cornelius Vanderbilt* (New York: Vintage Books, 2010), 369–96, for an explana-

tion of the complicated maneuvering and counterplotting involved in the "Harlem Corner."

26. "The Hon. John Morrissey: An Interview with Him at the Fifth Avenue Hotel," *Wheeling Daily Intelligencer,* Jan. 5, 1867. According to this article, which originally ran in the *Cincinnati Commercial* and was widely reprinted across the country, Morrissey recalled 1862 as the year he first lost in the stock market as a result of Vanderbilt's maneuverings. Vanderbilt had been quietly acquiring shares in Harlem Railroad stock for months, so it is possible that Morrissey had bought short early on in the stock's rise. Otherwise, and just as likely, it was 1863, when Vanderbilt executed the first of two market corners of the Harlem Railroad stock. "Death of John Morrissey," *New York Times,* May 2, 1878, 1, says that he lost a great deal of money in the "great rise in Harlem in 1863, when the New York City Common Council thought to corner Vanderbilt by rescinding the city ordinance authorizing him to extend the Hudson River freight line." The *Times* went on to say that he "realized large sums of money" in Wall Street over the next three years.

27. "The Hon. John Morrissey: An Interview with Him at the Fifth Avenue Hotel," *Wheeling Daily Intelligencer,* Jan. 5, 1867, citing the *Cincinnati Commercial.*

28. A famous line that Vanderbilt probably never actually wrote, but that nevertheless was repeated in his *New York Times* obituary, illustrates Vanderbilt's reputation for dealing with rivals: "Gentlemen: You have undertaken to cheat me. I won't sue, for the law is too slow. I'll ruin you. Yours truly, Cornelius Vanderbilt." Morrissey would eventually have a falling out with Vanderbilt and reportedly later said of the Commodore, "I have known in my life burglars, fighting men, and loafers, but never have I known such a bad fellow as Commodore Vanderbilt." Prior to the end of their friendship, however, the Commodore was instrumental in furthering the interests of John Morrissey and Saratoga Race Course. *New York Herald,* May 2, 1878.

29. *Statutes at Large of the State of New York,* edited by John W. Edmonds, 5 vols. (Albany, N.Y.: W. C. Little, 1863–90), 88th Session, Chap. 155, passed Mar. 21, 1865.

30. "Great Prospects for Saratoga," *Spirit of the Times,* Aug. 23, 1863; *Clearfield (Pa.) Republican,* Sept. 9, 1863; Hotaling, *They're Off!,* 50.

31. *New York Times,* Dec. 27, 1863.

32. Hotaling, *They're Off!,* 48; "The Watering Places," *New York*

Times, Jun. 19, 1864, 1. See also Violet B. Dunn, ed. *Saratoga County Heritage* (Saratoga County, N.Y., 1974), 157–58.

33. "The Turf," *New York Times,* Jul. 22, 1864, 7.

34. *New York Times,* Aug. 4, 1864. The *Times* called the racetrack "as level as a billiard table." Track management would proudly disagree with the claim that the track was level. In fact, it had banked turns, precisely calculated and constructed. The Travers was contested at one and three-quarter miles until 1889. It has been run at one and one-quarter miles since 1904. For further descriptions of the new track and the first race meet held there, see *New York Clipper,* Aug. 13, 1864.

35. "The Saratoga Racing Meeting," *New York Times,* Aug. 8, 1864.

36. Hotaling, *They're Off!,* 60–61.

37. "Saratoga Springs," *New York Times,* Jul. 9, 1865. The *Times* assured its readers that the track was "owned by a few wealthy gentlemen, who originally designed [it], and who have succeeded thus far in freeing it of all the objectionable features so conspicuous elsewhere. The names of the [in]corporators is sufficient guarantee that nothing improper will be tolerated. To secure this end, John Morrissey has been given the management, under the directors, of the whole place, and last season the grounds were visited by whole families."

38. "Saratoga," *New York Times,* Jul. 19, 1865. The genetic distinction between Standardbred trotters and Thoroughbred runners was not then as clear as it would become by the twentieth century.

39. *New York Times,* Aug. 8, 1865. Before the races, Dr. Underwood sold $70,000 worth of auction pools, and thousands more were doubtless bet in the betting ring near the grandstand on race days.

40. *New York Times,* Aug. 11, 1865.

41. "Scenes and Incidents at the Saratoga Races," *New York Times,* Aug. 10, 1865. The three top finishers in the 1865 Travers Stakes were, remarkably, all fillies sired by Lexington.

42. "The Turf," *New York Times,* Jul. 28, 1866.

43. "The Saratoga Race Meeting—Second Day—The Cup Day," *New York Times,* Jul. 27, 1866.

5. Congressman

1. *Indianapolis State Sentinel,* Aug. 30, 1865, citing the *Troy Times; Wheeling Daily Intelligencer,* Jul. 27, 1866.

2. "John Morrissey Accepts the Democratic Nomination for Congress," *New York Times*, Oct. 28, 1866. See also "Anti-Morrissey Meeting," *New York Times*, Oct. 30, 1866; *Washington National Republican*, Nov. 5, 1866.

3. *Wheeling Daily Intelligencer*, Nov. 1, 1866; "Not Fit to Be Made," *Vermont Watchman and State Journal*, Oct. 26, 1866, citing the *New York Tribune*.

4. *Vinton (Ohio) Record*, Dec. 6, 1866.

5. "John Morrissey and the Democracy," *Wheeling Daily Intelligencer*, Oct. 31, 1866, citing the *Newark Daily Advertiser*.

6. *Memphis Public Ledger*, Oct. 20, 1866, citing the *Louisville Courier*.

7. *Urbana Union*, Nov. 28, 1866.

8. *New York Tribune*, Nov. 5, 1866.

9. *Philadelphia Evening Telegraph*, Nov. 12, 1866.

10. *New York Times*, Nov. 5, 1866, 4.

11. *Holt County (Mo.) Sentinel*, Dec. 14, 1866. The newspaper noted: "John Morrissey, the Copperhead bruiser and blackleg, was elected to Congress by the following vote: Morrissey, Copperhead, 9,159; Taylor, decent Democrat, 6,451; Elliott, Republican, 2,292. Morrissey's majority, 2,708 over Taylor, and 416 over both opponents."

12. *(Hillsborough, Ohio) Highland Weekly News*, Dec. 6, 1866.

13. *Zion's Herald and Wesleyan Journal*, Dec. 19, 1866.

14. *Ashtabula (Ohio) Weekly Telegraph*, Nov. 10, 1866.

15. Marcus "Brick" Pomeroy, *Memphis Public Ledger*, Dec. 12, 1866. For a summary of the life and career of Pomeroy, see his obituary in the *New York Times*, May 31, 1896.

16. "Morrissey: A Pen Picture of the Pugilistic Congressman," *Memphis Public Ledger*, Nov. 26, 1866, citing the *Cincinnati Commercial*.

17. "A Monkey Biting John Morrissey's Boy," *Philadelphia Evening Telegraph*, Oct. 19, 1866, citing the *New York Evening Post*.

18. *Philadelphia Evening Telegraph*, Nov. 20, 1866. The *Charleston Daily News*, Oct. 11, 1867, described a sighting of Mrs. Morrissey in Manhattan: "The weather being unusually fine yesterday, Fifth Avenue was a sight to behold, and reminded one of the Boulevards of the great French capital. The loveliest woman of them all was Mrs. John Morrissey, wife of the distinguished ex-prize fighter, faro-dealer, and member of Congress—who would himself be good looking enough were it not for the memento of affection imprinted upon his nasal pro-

tuberance by John C. Heenan, which rather mars its symmetry. Mrs. Morrissey's wardrobe would purchase one of the best localities in the city, and, as to her beauty—[the poet's] feeble pen cannot do justice to the charms of the strong man's much better half."

19. *Nashville Union and Dispatch,* Mar. 27, 1868; *Fremont (Ohio) Weekly Journal,* Apr. 3, 1868, citing the *Troy Times.*

20. *Wheeling Daily Intelligencer,* Jul. 6, 1867, citing the *New York Home Journal.*

21. *Wheeling Daily Intelligencer,* Jun. 26, 1867.

22. For example, see *Lancaster (Ohio) Gazette,* Nov. 22, 1866; *Washington National Republican,* Nov. 27, 1866; "Generous," *Washington Evening Star,* Jan. 19, 1867; *Philadelphia Evening Telegraph,* Mar. 24, 1869, 8. The *St. Johnsberry (Vt.) Caledonian,* Oct. 9, 1863, reported that "John Morrissey, of pugilistic fame, lately gave $500 to a Troy chambermaid who was honest enough to give John a package of $7000 which he had left under his pillow." Morrissey seemed to have a problem leaving large amounts of cash in his bedding because a similar story circulated in 1871, crediting Morrissey with giving "$500 to a chambermaid at Albany who took care of $26,000, which he left under his pillow in his room." *Terre-Haute Weekly Express,* Mar. 22, 1871.

23. "John Morrissey in Congress," *New York Times,* Mar. 6, 1867.

24. *New York Times,* Apr. 17, 1867.

25. *Memphis Daily Appeal,* Apr. 19, 1871, 3.

26. *Ashtabula (Ohio) Weekly Telegraph,* Dec. 8, 1866.

27. *New York Sun,* Dec. 9, 1869.

28. "John Morrissey in Congress," *New York Times,* Mar. 6, 1867, 4; "The Assembling of the Fortieth Congress," *Charleston Daily News,* Mar. 8, 1867.

29. *Charleston Daily News,* Mar. 11, 1867.

30. *The Monthly Religious Magazine,* Feb. 1868, 132; *Memphis Public Ledger,* Mar. 7, 1868; Paul H. Bergeron, ed., *The Papers of Andrew Johnson,* vol. 14: *April–August 1868* (Knoxville: University of Tennessee Press, 1997), xiv.

31. "John Morrissey," *Vermont Daily Transcript,* Sept. 15, 1868, citing the *New York Sun.*

32. *Memphis Public Ledger,* Dec. 5, 1868. James McCurlin was the losing Republican candidate. A blurb in the *White Cloud (Kan.) Chief,* Nov. 8, 1866, alleged that "John Morrissey, in view of a seat

in Congress, and no prospective draft, has condescended to become a citizen of the United States. His final naturalization papers are dated October 11, 1866."

33. *Tarboro (N.C.) Southerner,* Mar. 11, 1869.

34. *New Orleans Crescent,* Mar. 16, 1869.

35. *Memphis Daily Appeal,* Oct. 2, 1869.

36. *New York Times,* Oct. 5, 1869.

37. *Charleston Daily News,* Jul. 19, 1870. The *Burlington Weekly Free Press,* Jul. 22, 1870, reported: "237 times he failed to respond when his vote was wanted."

38. *Memphis Public Ledger,* Jan. 28, 1870.

39. "The Useless Member," *New York Times,* May 4, 1870.

40. See Charles F. Wingate, "An Episode in Municipal Government: The Reign of the Ring," *North American Review,* Jan. 1875, 119.

41. The Young Democracy won over a majority of the General Committee of Tammany Hall but failed to capture the Tammany Society, where they were soundly defeated. They ran a ticket of officers including John Fox, Samuel Tilden, John Morrissey, and Augustus Schell but received only 23 votes to 250 for the Tweed ticket. See *New York Tribune,* Apr. 19, 1870. See also "Failed Young Democracy Coup: Morrissey and Other Tweed-Sweeney Ring Opponents Making a Push for Control of the Party," *New York Tribune,* Mar. 28, 1870.

42. Morrissey was nominated for a third term by the Young Democracy, according to the *Knoxville Daily Chronicle,* Oct. 23, 1870. That nomination doomed a possible alliance with Republicans against the Tammany Democrats. Morrissey declined the nomination, according to the *Columbia Daily Phoenix,* Nov. 6, 1870, but the *New York Tribune,* Nov. 8, 1870, said that he would run as an independent candidate. Any campaign that was mounted on Morrissey's behalf was brief and unsuccessful.

43. See "Hon. John Morrissey at Jem Mace's Saloon—A Bloody Fight Prevented," *New York Times,* Dec. 31, 1870, 2; *New York Times,* Jan. 1, 1871, 5.

6. Impresario

1. *Memphis Daily Appeal,* Apr. 19, 1871, 3. According to tales that drifted back upriver, his trip down the Mississippi was eventful in

that he was rumored to have saved a woman from a bear that had escaped from its cage atop the boat by grabbing a rope attached to the animal's neck. See *Memphis Public Ledger,* Apr. 3, 1871, 4.

2. *Memphis Daily Appeal,* Apr. 17, 1871, 4. The *Nashville Union and American,* Apr. 23, 1871, 3, and *Charleston Daily News,* Apr. 26, 1871, 2, claimed that the purchase price was $4,000. The price named in the *Daily Appeal* was $10,000.

3. *(New York) Independent,* Jul. 21, 1870; *New York Evangelist,* Jul. 14, 1870, 1. An article titled "A Princely Gambling Hell," in the *Columbia (S.C.) Daily Phoenix,* Jun. 28, 1870, described the house as follows: "John Morrissey's new house there is far the most gorgeous house for play on the continent. The main floor is divided into three rooms; two of which are devoted to play and one for dining. The fitting up of the rooms is simply magnificent. The floors are covered with scarlet and white velvet tapestry. The furniture, side-boards, cornices, mantels and mirror frames are French chavel, inlaid with gold. The curtains are silk and damask. The monogram 'J.M.' flames out on all sides. Over the massive mirrors are carved tigers' heads, with mouths wide open to devour, an emblem of the tiger persons will fight within the walls. The chandeliers are gold gilt, and the brackets are burnished in the same style. Private staircases lead to rooms aloft, and these rooms, on the stories above the parlors, are gorgeously fitted up for guests. The lower floor is for kitchen, wine cellar, laundry and for domestic uses."

4. *Massachusetts Ploughman and New England Journal of Agriculture,* Jul. 15, 1871, 2. The *Fairfield (S.C.) Herald,* Jun. 28, 1871, contains a more detailed description of the renovation: "A new addition to the palace is represented as truly gorgeous. It is fifty by seventy-five feet, and one story high, making it the largest room of the kind in the world. It is lighted by immense skylights, and side lights as well; the windows reaching from the ceiling to the floor, twenty-two feet. All the wood work in this grand salon is of solid black walnut, beautifully (and suggestively) carved in tiger's heads and all kinds of fancy ornamentation. The fifty yards of carpet covering the room is a French moquette, costing $6 per yard. The furniture is correspondingly gorgeous, all of walnut, richly inlaid with gilt, and upholstered in moquette of crimson and gold. Tigers' heads, with mouths wide open, displaying rows of golden teeth, are carved in the backs of the chairs and sofas, and the gaming tables are ornamented in a similar way. These latter are of rose-

wood, most beautifully carved and gilded. A solid silver roulette wheel will be placed in the room with other gaming implements. Massive bronzes and other expensive ornaments are scattered around the saloon in the greatest profusion, and the whole appearance of the apartment is grand in the extreme. This is the den proper of the tiger. Other parts of the building are arranged with equal disregard to expense."

5. *Memphis Public Ledger,* Aug. 7, 1870. That year Morrissey reportedly sold a portion of his interest in the casino to a partnership of Charles Reed and Albert Spencer, the two men who would own, with Morrissey, the Saratoga Race Course at the time of Morrissey's death.

6. *Memphis Public Ledger,* Aug. 27, 1873, 2.

7. *Tifflin (Ohio) Tribune,* Jul. 28, 1870, quoting a *New York Sun* correspondent.

8. *Washington Evening Star,* Sept. 6, 1870; *New York Evangelist,* Jul. 14, 1870.

9. *New York Tribune,* Jun. 27, 1871, 4.

10. "Saratoga Out of Season: Evidence of Permanent Prosperity in the Place," *New York Times,* May 4, 1874, 5.

11. "How Morrissey Checkmated the Thieves," *Ogdensburg (N.Y.) Journal,* Jul. 25, 1870.

12. Kent Hollingsworth, *The Kentucky Thoroughbred* (Lexington: University Press of Kentucky, 1985), 74–75.

13. Edward Hotaling, *They're Off! Horse Racing at Saratoga* (Syracuse, N.Y.: Syracuse University Press, 1995), 90–91. For an interesting tale of murder most foul involving Harper's family, see Maryjean Wall, *How Kentucky Became Southern: A Talk of Outlaws, Horse Thieves, Gamblers, and Breeders* (Lexington: University Press of Kentucky, 2010), 98–100.

14. Hollingsworth, *The Kentucky Thoroughbred,* 76; *Woodsfield (Ohio) Spirit of Democracy,* Jul. 25, 1871, 2; see also "The Great Race for the Saratoga Cup," *New York Times,* Jul. 15, 1871.

15. *New York Times,* Jul. 18, 1871; *Sacramento Daily Union,* Jul. 24, 1871.

16. *Charleston Daily News,* Jul. 20, 1871, 1. Other clockers, including Captain William Cottrill, had the mile time as fast as 1:39.

17. The team's official name was The Union Club of Lansingburgh, New York. The village of Lansingburgh would later be subsumed by the city of Troy.

18. See Tom Melville, *Early Baseball and the Rise of the National League* (Jefferson, N.C.: McFarland, 2001), 10–22. Foreign-born players became increasingly prevalent in the new professional environment, and immigrants formed an important part of the fan base of early commercialized baseball, which provided an opportunity for social interaction and cultural assimilation for immigrant sports enthusiasts.

19. Harry Ellard, *Base Ball in Cincinnati: A History* (1907; Jefferson, N.C.: McFarland, 2004), 105.

20. See Robert E. Burke, *Never Just a Game: Players, Owners, and American Baseball to 1920* (Chapel Hill: University of North Carolina Press, 1994), 30.

21. See Christopher Devine, *Harry Wright: The Father of Professional Baseball* (Jefferson, N.C.: McFarland, 2003), 57.

22. See Ellard, *Base Ball in Cincinnati*, 115; Devine, *Harry Wright*, 57.

23. Months later the teams made amends after Troy issued a written apology in exchange for its share of the game's gate receipts. In 1871 the Haymakers became a founding member of the first American professional sports league, the National Association of Professional Base Ball Players, while the Cincinnati club, faced with mounting debt, disbanded (later to reform as charter members of the National League). The Reds would be expelled from the National League in 1880 for selling beer on Sundays but would rejoin the league in 1890.

24. John H. Davis, *The American Turf* (New York: J. Polhemus, 1907), 129 (quotes); William H. P. Robertson, *The History of Thoroughbred Racing in America* (Englewood Cliffs, N.J.: Prentice-Hall, 1964), 108. See also Katherine C. Mooney, *Race Horse Men: How Slavery and Freedom Were Made at the Racetrack* (Cambridge, Mass.: Harvard University Press, 2014), 114.

25. See Steven A. Riess, *The Sport of Kings and the Kings of Crime: Horse Racing, Politics, and Organized Crime in New York, 1865–1913* (Syracuse, N.Y.: Syracuse University Press, 2011), 102.

26. "The Great Race," *New York Times,* Jul. 3, 1872.

27. "The Great Race," *New York Times,* Jul. 3, 1872. As the jockeys were being hoisted up onto their mounts, a passerby showed Longfellow's jockey, an African American named Joe Sample, a fifty-dollar bill and said, "You win, and you get this." The *Times* reported that "the darkey smiled pleasantly and showed his white teeth as he looked

at his master as if to say, 'I'll take it, but I win for massa's sake,'" a reminder of the vestiges of slavery that survived in horse racing long after the end of the Civil War and the passage of the Thirteenth Amendment. For further reading on the disappearance of once-prominent black jockeys from American racetracks, see Edward Hotaling, *The Great Black Jockeys* (Rocklin, Calif.: Forum, 1999), and Mooney, *Race Horse Men.*

28. "The Great Race," *New York Times,* Jul. 3, 1872.

29. "There never was a contest in America which was witnessed by such extraordinary numbers," according to the *New York Times,* Jul. 3, 1872. Estimates of the size of the crowd ran as high as forty thousand, but twenty-five thousand seems to be a more reasonable number.

30. "The Great Race," *New York Times,* Jul. 3, 1872.

31. "The Greatest Contest in American Turf History," *New York Times,* Jul. 17, 1872.

32. "The Greatest Contest in American Turf History," *New York Times,* Jul. 17, 1872. Bowie's most significant contribution to American racing was the fact that he was indirectly responsible for the creation of the Preakness Stakes, the foundation for which was laid at a dinner party in 1868 in Saratoga hosted by Milton H. Sanford, who had made a fortune manufacturing blankets for the Union army during the Civil War. In the course of the party a group of men, including Saratoga Association executive John Hunter, decided to organize a stakes race to which they would all nominate their top horses. Bowie convinced the group to hold the race in Baltimore and promised to contribute $15,000 to the purse. He then convinced the Maryland Jockey Club to construct a racetrack, which would be named Pimlico. The winner of the Dinner Party Stakes, owned by Sanford, was a colt named Preakness, for whom the Preakness Stakes is named. The first Preakness Stakes was won by John Chamberlain's colt Survivor, who prevailed by ten lengths—a record that would last for 132 years before Smarty Jones eclipsed the mark in 2004.

33. *Washington Evening Star,* Jul. 17, 1872.

34. "The Greatest Contest in American Turf History," *New York Times,* Jul. 17, 1872.

35. "The Greatest Contest in American Turf History," *New York Times,* Jul. 17, 1872.

36. "The Greatest Contest in American Turf History," *New York Times,* Jul. 17, 1872.

37. *Washington Evening Star,* Jul. 17, 1872; "The Greatest Contest in American Turf History," *New York Times,* Jul. 17, 1872.

38. See Jim Bolus, *Derby Dreams* (Gretna, La.: Pelican, 1996), 86–87; "A Noted Horseman Dead," *New York Times,* Feb. 15, 1887.

39. *New York Times,* Jul. 20, 1872.

40. *Nashville Union and American,* Aug. 18, 1872, 1.

41. See Hotaling, *They're Off!,* 110–11.

42. "America Victorious," *New York Times,* Sept. 12, 1871.

43. *Boston Daily Advertiser,* Sept. 16, 1873.

44. *Saratoga Springs Saratogian,* Mar. 19, 1874, citing the *(New York) Independent,* Jan. 29, 1874, 17.

45. "The Saratoga Regatta Course," *Forest and Stream,* Mar. 12, 1874, 77.

46. *Daily Cleveland Herald,* Jan. 24, 1874.

47. "The Unrowed Race," *New York Times,* Jul. 18, 1874; *Chicago Inter Ocean,* Jul. 18, 1874, 2. Despite agreements of local drivers not to gouge the tourists, reports of exorbitant fares were widely circulated.

48. *Chicago Inter Ocean,* Jul. 22, 1874.

49. "From Saratoga," *Chicago Inter Ocean,* Aug. 2, 1874, 6. See "A Victory for Columbia," *New York Times,* Jul. 19, 1874, and "The Contest Reviewed," *New York Times,* Jul. 20, 1874, 2, for a discussion of the race, the results, claims of foul, and betting.

50. *Chicago Inter Ocean,* Jul. 22, 1874; "The Unrowed Race," *New York Times,* Jul. 18, 1874.

51. Hotaling, *They're Off!,* 103.

52. See Samuel Crowther, *Rowing and Track Athletics* (New York: Macmillan, 1905). In 1875 the regatta expanded to thirteen teams. Bowdoin, Brown, and Amherst joined the regatta, the latter of which had boycotted the previous year's event in protest of Morrissey and gambling.

7. Vindication

1. "Our Proofs of Fraud against the City Government," *New York Times,* Jul. 24, 1871. See Gustavus Myers, *The History of Tammany Hall* (New York: Boni and Liveright, 1917), 240–48. The *New York Evening Post,* Nov. 6, 1871, estimated that the Tweed Ring stole $59 million. The *New York Times,* Nov. 7, 1871, placed the number

at $75–80 million. See also Alexander B. Callow Jr., *The Tweed Ring* (New York: Oxford University Press, 1966), 164–83.

2. William E. Harding, *John Morrissey, His Life, Battles, and Wrangles, from His Birth in Ireland until He Died a State Senator* (New York, 1881), 290.

3. "Shall Morrissey Rule?," *New York Times*, Oct. 27, 1873, 1.

4. *New York Times*, Nov. 8, 1873. For a time, Morrissey and Kelly were political comrades, as illustrated by a physical altercation in a New York City barroom between Morrissey and a vocal critic of Kelly that left the man with a broken nose and two black eyes. "Those who are skilled in such affairs say he will not be able to appear in public for some days," said the *New York Times*, Sept. 23, 1874.

5. "Short-Hairs versus Swallow-Tails," *New York Times*, Jun. 16, 1875, 10.

6. "John Morrissey's Treason," *New York Times*, Jun. 22, 1875, 7; *New York Times*, Jun. 20, 1875, 2; *New York Times*, Jun. 21, 1875, 8; *New York Times*, Jul. 25, 1875, 12. Days later Morrissey sought to appear before the General Committee to plead his case, but Kelly threatened to use his influence as the functional "landlord" of the meeting house to bar him. *New York Times*, Jul. 28, 1875, 8.

7. "John Morrissey's Return," *New York Times*, Sept. 4, 1875, 8.

8. "Fourth Senatorial District," *New York Times*, Oct. 17, 1875, 2.

9. "The Duty of the Hour," *New York Times*, Oct. 22, 1875, 5.

10. "A Probable Political Murder," *New York Times*, Oct. 23, 1875, 5.

11. "The Fox-Morrissey Contest," *New York Times*, Oct. 26, 1875, 1.

12. "Bad Man to Elect," *New York Times*, Oct. 26, 1875, 1.

13. "Anti-Tammany Meetings," *New York Times*, Oct. 26, 1877.

14. "Morrissey's Campaign," *New York Times*, Oct. 30, 1875, 12.

15. "John Morrissey's Victory," *New York Times*, Nov. 3, 1875, 2.

16. "More about Cipher Dispatches," *New York Times*, Dec. 7, 1878, 1. See also *Harper's Weekly*, Feb. 24, 1877, with a cartoon on its cover depicting Morrissey buying swine, which he reportedly claimed was as easy as buying electors.

17. The commission consisted of five appointees from the House (three Democrats, two Republicans), five from the Senate (three Republicans, two Democrats), and five from the Supreme Court. The Su-

preme Court delegation was composed of two Democratic and two Republican justices, and those four chose the fifth commissioner, a relative independent named Joseph P. Bradley, a Grant appointee, who ultimately cast the deciding vote.

18. See "Swindling Pool Sellers," *New York Times*, Dec. 15, 1876, 2; *New York Times*, Dec. 10, 1876, 1; *New York Times*, Dec. 11, 1876, 1; *New York Times*, Dec. 12, 1876, 1. The *Anderson (S.C.) Court House Intelligencer*, Dec. 7, 1876, was critical of the popular practice of betting on election results: "Betting men would pursue their business even to wagers on the day of judgment, if the event were not to be of a character precluding payment." By the early twentieth century, some were claiming that Morrissey had sold $2 million in bets on the 1876 election. See "Law's Distinction in Methods of Gambling," *New York Times*, Apr. 19, 1901.

19. " John Morrissey, Jr.'s Majority," *New York Times*, Aug. 11, 1876; "Injury to John Morrissey's Son," *New York Times*, Sept. 6, 1873; "John Morrissey, Jr., Blown Up," *Saratoga Sentinel*, Sept. 11, 1873; "Accident to John Morrissey, Jr.," *Washington Evening Star*, Sept. 6, 1873.

20. *Easton (Ohio) Democrat*, Jan. 11, 1877, citing the *New York Tribune*; see also "Death of Young Morrissey," *Memphis Public Ledger*, Jan. 8, 1877.

21. *New York Sun*, May 2, 1878.

22. "An Address to Electors," *New York Times*, Oct. 28, 1877.

23. "Indorsing Senator Morrissey," *New York Times*, Oct. 30, 1877.

24. For a summary of Morrissey's legislative accomplishments in Albany, see *New York Times*, Nov. 1, 1877.

25. "On Trial for Manslaughter," *New York Times*, Nov. 8, 1878. A week before the election, the man who had shot a critic of Morrissey's in a pre-election fracas two years earlier found himself in a similar situation, but this time he was defending Morrissey's opponent. Edwin Haggerty, a backer of Schell, was sitting in a cigar store on Broadway when a Morrissey supporter staggered through the entrance and boldly predicted that Morrissey would win by more votes than Schell would receive. The man offered to bet Haggerty, who gladly accepted. As Haggerty turned to leave the store for the saloon at the rear of the building, the drunk man struck Haggerty in the face. In the course of their ensuing tussle, the pair crashed through the glass partition that separated

the cigar store from the barroom, injuring both severely. See "Vigorous Political Argument," *New York Times,* Oct. 31, 1877.

26. See "Illness of Senator Morrissey," *New York Times,* Oct. 10, 1877, 5.

27. "Local Political Matters," *New York Times,* Nov. 2, 1877, 2, 5. Morrissey and Schell had done business together, participating in stock-trading ventures, and apparently there was no bad blood between them on a personal level. Morrissey felt that his real opponent was Kelly.

28. "Four Speeches for Morrissey," *New York Times,* Nov. 3, 1877, 5. Morrissey managed to attend only two of the eleven rallies held in his honor the next night, where his "remarks were frequently interrupted with cheers and applause" from the large gatherings.

29. "An Address from John Morrissey," *New York Times,* Nov. 5, 1877, 5.

30. "The Seventh Senate District," *New York Times,* Nov. 6, 1877; "Senator Morrissey's Victory," *New York Times,* Nov. 7, 1877; "Election Day Incidents," *New York Times,* Nov. 7, 1877.

31. "Senator Morrissey's Victory," *New York Times,* Nov. 7, 1877.

32. *Christian Union,* Nov. 14, 1877, 415.

33. "John Morrissey's Victory," *New York Times,* Nov. 8, 1877.

34. "Senator Morrissey's Health Trip," *New York Times,* Nov. 16, 1877.

35. "Condition of Hon. John Morrissey," *New York Times,* Jan. 16, 1878, 1; "Hon. John Morrissey Dying," *New York Times,* Jan. 17, 1878, 5.

36. "Senator Morrissey Improving," *New York Times,* Jan. 22, 1878, 1.

37. *New York Sun,* May 2, 1878; "Death of John Morrissey," *New York Daily Tribune,* May 2, 1878.

38. "Death of John Morrissey," *New York Times,* May 2, 1878, 1.

39. "Mourned by Thousands," *New York Times,* May 3, 1878, 1.

40. *National Police Gazette,* May 11, 1878, 2.

41. "Saratoga's Race Season," *New York Times,* Jul. 20, 1878, 5 (quote). See also, "John Morrissey's Estate," *New York Times,* May 11, 1878; "John Morrissey's Executors," *New York Times,* Mar. 28, 1880; "John Morrissey's Will Recalled," *New York Times,* Dec. 17, 1880.

Bibliography

Adelman, Melvin L. *A Sporting Time: New York City and the Rise of Modern Athletics, 1820–1870.* Urbana: University of Illinois Press, 1986.

Allen, Lee. *The Cincinnati Reds.* New York: G. P. Putnam's Sons, 1948.

Anbinder, Tyler. *Five Points: The 19th-Century New York City Neighborhood That Invented Tap Dance, Stole Elections, and Became the World's Most Notorious Slum.* New York: Plume, 2002.

Anderson, James Douglas. *Making the American Thoroughbred: Especially in Tennessee, 1800–1845.* Norwood, Mass.: Plimpton, 1916.

Armstead, Myra B. Young. *"Lord Please Don't Take Me in August": African-Americans in Newport and Saratoga Springs, 1820–1930.* Urbana: University of Illinois Press, 1999.

Asbury, Herbert. *Gangs of New York: An Informal History of the Underworld.* New York: Alfred A. Knopf, 1927.

———. *Sucker's Progress: An Informal History of Gambling in America.* New York: Thunder's Mouth, 2003. (Orig. pub. 1938.)

Bartles, Jon. *Saratoga Stories: Gangsters, Gamblers, and Racing Legends.* Lexington, Ky.: Eclipse, 2007.

Bergeron, Paul H., ed. *The Papers of Andrew Johnson.* Vol. 14: *April–August 1868.* Knoxville: University of Tennessee Press, 1997.

Bolus, Jim. *Derby Dreams.* Gretna, La.: Pelican, 1996.

Bradley, Hugh. *Such Was Saratoga.* New York: Doubleday, Doran and Company, 1940.

Breen, Matthew Patrick. *Thirty Years of New York Politics Up-to-Date.* New York: Matthew P. Breen, 1899.

Briggs, Emily Edson. *The Olivia Letters; Being Some History of Washington City for Forty Years by the Letters of a Newspaper Correspondent.* New York: Neale, 1906.

Brown, Dona. *Inventing New England: Regional Tourism in the Nineteenth Century*. Washington, D.C.: Smithsonian Institution Press, 1995.

Brown, Roscoe C. E., and Ray B. Smith. *Political and Governmental History of the State of New York*. Vol. 3. Syracuse, N.Y.: Syracuse Press, 1922.

Burke, Robert E. *Never Just a Game: Players, Owners, and American Baseball to 1920*. Chapel Hill: University of North Carolina Press, 1994.

Burrows, Edwin G., and Mike Wallace. *Gotham: A History of New York City to 1898*. New York: Oxford University Press, 1999.

Callow, Alexander B., Jr. *The Tweed Ring*. New York: Oxford University Press, 1966.

Campbell, Tracy. *Deliver the Vote: A History of Election Fraud, an American Political Tradition—1742–2004*. New York: Carroll and Graf, 2005.

Case, Carleton B. *Humor of Abraham Lincoln, Gathered from Authentic Sources*. Chicago: Shrewesbury, 1916.

Chafetz, Henry. *Play the Devil: A History of Gambling in the United States from 1492 to 1955*. London: Forgotten Books, 2013. (Orig. pub. 1960.)

Chambers, Thomas A. *Drinking the Waters: Creating an American Leisure Class at Nineteenth-Century Mineral Springs*. Washington, D.C.: Smithsonian Institution Press, 2002.

Cliff, Nigel. *The Shakespeare Riots: Revenge, Drama, and Death in Nineteenth-Century New York*. New York: Random House, 2007.

Corbett, Theodore. *The Making of American Resorts: Saratoga Springs, Ballston Spa, Lake George*. New Brunswick, N.J.: Rutgers University Press, 2001.

Crowther, Samuel. *Rowing and Track Athletics*. New York: Macmillan, 1905.

Davies, Richard O. *Sports in American Life: A History*. Hoboken, N.J.: Wiley-Blackwell, 2012.

Davis, John H. *The American Turf: History of the Thoroughbred, Together with Personal Reminiscences by the Author, Who, in Turn, Has Been Jockey Trainer and Owner*. New York: John Polhemus Printing Company, 1907.

Devine, Christopher. *Harry Wright: The Father of Professional Baseball*. Jefferson, N.C.: McFarland, 2003.

Bibliography

Diner, Hasia R. *Erin's Daughters in America: Irish Immigrant Women in the Nineteenth Century*. Baltimore: Johns Hopkins University Press, 1983.

Dizikes, John. *Sportsmen and Gentlemen: From the Years That Shaped American Ideas about Winning and Losing and How to Play the Game*. Boston: Houghton Mifflin, 1981.

———. *Yankee Doodle Dandy: The Life and Times of Tod Sloan*. New Haven: Yale University Press, 2000.

Dreistadt, Ronnie. *Lost Bluegrass: History of a Vanishing Landscape*. Charleston: History Press, 2011.

Dunkelman, Mark H. *Patrick Henry Jones: Irish American, Civil War General, and Gilded Age Politician*. Baton Rouge: Louisiana State University Press, 2015.

Dunn, Violet B., ed. *Saratoga County Heritage*. Saratoga County, N.Y., 1974.

Eisenberg, John. *The Great Match Race: When North Met South in America's First Sports Spectacle*. Boston: Houghton Mifflin, 2006.

Ellard, Harry. *Base Ball in Cincinnati: A History*. Jefferson, N.C.: McFarland, 2004. (Orig. pub. 1907.)

Erie, Steven P. *Rainbow's End: Irish-Americans and the Dilemmas of Urban Machine Politics, 1840–1985*. Berkeley: University of California Press, 1988.

Feeney, Vincent Edward. "Pre-famine Irish in Vermont, 1815–1844." *Vermont History* 74 (Summer/Fall 2006): 101–26.

Gammie, Peter. "Pugilists and Politicians in Antebellum New York: The Life and Times of Tom Hyer." *New York History* 75, no. 3 (July 1994): 265–97.

Gassan, Richard. *The Birth of American Tourism: New York, the Hudson Valley, and American Culture, 1790–1830*. Amherst: University of Massachusetts Press, 2008.

Gildea, Dennis. "'Cross-Counter': The Heenan-Morrissey Fight of 1858 and Frank Queen's Attack on the 'Respectable Press.'" *Colby Quarterly* 32, no. 1 (1996): 11–22.

Golway, Terry. *Machine Made: Tammany Hall and the Creation of Modern American Politics*. New York: Norton, 2014.

Gordon, Michael A. *The Orange Riots: Political Violence in New York City, 1870 and 1871*. Ithaca, N.Y.: Cornell University Press, 1993.

Gorn, Elliott J. "'Good-Bye Boys, I Die a True American': Homicide,

Nativism, and Working-Class Culture in Antebellum New York City." *Journal of American History* 74, no. 2 (September 1987): 388–410.

———. *The Manly Art: Bare-Knuckle Prize Fighting in America*. Ithaca, N.Y.: Cornell University Press, 1986.

Harding, William E. *John Morrissey, His Life, Battles, and Wrangles, from His Birth in Ireland until He Died a State Senator*. New York, 1881. (Published serially in the *Police Gazette*.)

Headley, J. T. *The Great Riots of New York, 1712 to 1873*. New York: E. B. Treat, 1873.

Heimer, Mel. *Fabulous Bawd: The Story of Saratoga*. Saratoga Springs, N.Y.: Holt, 1952.

Hollingsworth, Kent. *The Kentucky Thoroughbred*. Lexington: University Press of Kentucky, 2011.

Hone, Philip. *The Diaries of Philip Hone*. Vol. 1. Ithaca, N.Y.: Cornell University Library, 2014.

Hotaling, Edward. *The Great Black Jockeys: The Lives and Times of the Men Who Dominated America's First National Sport*. Rocklin, Calif.: Forum, 1999.

———. *They're Off! Horse Racing at Saratoga*. Syracuse, N.Y.: Syracuse University Press, 1995.

James, Ed, ed. *Life and Battles of Yankee Sullivan*. New York: Ed James, 1880.

Johnson, H., ed. *The American Fistiana*. New York: H. Johnson, 1849.

Kingsdale, Jon M. "The 'Poor Man's Club': Social Functions of the Urban Working-Class Saloon." *American Quarterly* 25, no. 4 (October 1973): 472–89.

Kurutz, Gary F. "Popular Culture on the Golden Shore." In *Rooted in Barbarous Soil: People, Culture, and Community in Gold Rush California*, ed. Kevin Starr and Richard J. Orsi, 280–315. Berkeley: University of California Press, 2000.

Landau, Sarah Bradford, and Carl W. Condit. *Rise of the New York Skyscraper, 1865–1913*. New Haven, Conn.: Yale University Press, 1999.

Lane, Wheaton J. *Commodore Vanderbilt: An Epic of the Steam Age*. New York: Alfred A. Knopf, 1942.

Lears, Jackson. *Something for Nothing: Luck in America*. New York: Viking, 2003.

Lynch, Denis Tilden. *"Boss" Tweed: The Story of a Grim Generation.* New Brunswick, N.J.: Transaction, 2002.

Manning, Landon. *The Noble Animals: Tales of the Saratoga Turf.* Saratoga, N.Y.: Landon Manning, 1973.

McDaniels, Pellom, III. *The Prince of Jockeys: The Life of Isaac Burns Murphy.* Lexington: University Press of Kentucky, 2013.

McIntyre, Rebecca Caywood. *Souvenirs of the Old South: Northern Tourism and Southern Mythology.* Gainesville: University Press of Florida, 2011.

Melville, Tom. *Early Baseball and the Rise of the National League.* Jefferson, N.C.: McFarland, 2001.

Merwin, Henry Childs. *The Life of Bret Harte, with Some Account of the California Pioneers.* Boston: Houghton Mifflin, 1911.

Monkkonen, Eric H. *Murder in New York City.* Berkeley: University of California Press, 2000.

Mooney, Katherine C. *Race Horse Men: How Slavery and Freedom Were Made at the Racetrack.* Cambridge, Mass.: Harvard University Press, 2014.

———. "Race Horse Men: Slavery and Freedom at the Nineteenth-Century Racetrack." Ph.D. diss., Yale University, 2012.

Mushkat, Jerome. *Fernando Wood: A Political Biography.* Kent, Ohio: Kent State University Press, 1990.

Myers, Gustavus. *The History of Tammany Hall.* New York: Boni and Liveright, 1917.

Palmer, Joseph. *This Was Racing.* Lexington, Ky.: Henry Clay Press, 1973.

Parmer, Charles B. *For Gold and Glory: The Story of Thoroughbred Racing in America.* New York: Carrick and Evans, 1939.

Peterson, Harold. *The Man Who Invented Baseball.* New York: Charles Scribner's Sons, 1969.

Pleasants, Samuel Augustus. *Fernando Wood of New York.* New York: Columbia University Press, 1948.

Rader, Benjamin. *American Sports: From the Age of Folk Games to the Age of Televised Sports.* Englewood Cliffs, N.J.: Prentice Hall, 1990.

———. *Baseball: A History of America's Game.* Urbana: University of Illinois Press, 1992.

Redmond, Patrick R. *The Irish and the Making of American Sport, 1835–1920.* Jefferson, N.C.: McFarland, 2014.

Riess, Steven A. *Sport in Industrial America, 1850–1920.* Oxford: Wiley-Blackwell, 2013.

———. *The Sport of Kings and the Kings of Crime: Horse Racing, Politics, and Organized Crime in New York, 1865–1913.* Syracuse, N.Y.: Syracuse University Press, 2011.

Robertson, William H. P. *The History of Thoroughbred Racing in America.* Englewood Cliffs, N.J.: Prentice-Hall, 1964.

Roseler, Bob. *The Fair Grounds: Big Shots and Long Shots.* New Orleans: Arthur Hard Enterprises, 1998.

Roundtree, B. Seebohm, ed. *Betting and Gambling: A National Evil.* New York: Macmillan, 1905.

Rubin, Lucas G. *Brooklyn's Sportsmen's Row: Politics, Society, and the Sporting Life on Northern Eighth Avenue.* Charleston, S.C.: History Press, 2012.

Smith, Joseph Aubin. *Reminiscences of Saratoga.* New York: Knickerbocker, 1897.

Smith, Matthew Hale. *Sunshine and Shadow in New York.* Hartford: J. B. Burr and Company, 1868.

Smith, Red. "The First Belmont—A Horse." *New York Times,* June 9, 1974.

Smith, Ronald A. *Sports and Freedom: The Rise of Big-Time College Athletics.* New York: Oxford University Press, 1988.

Sterngass, Jon. *First Resorts: Pursuing Pleasure at Saratoga Springs, Newport, and Coney Island.* Baltimore: Johns Hopkins University Press, 2001.

Stiles, T. J. *The First Tycoon: The Epic Life of Cornelius Vanderbilt.* New York: Vintage Books, 2010.

Stott, Richard. *Jolly Fellows: Male Milieus in Nineteenth-Century America.* Baltimore: Johns Hopkins University Press, 2009.

Sylvester, Nathaniel Bartlett. *History of Saratoga County, New York.* Philadelphia: Everts and Ensign, 1878.

Trevathan, Charles E. *The American Thoroughbred.* New York: Macmillan, 1905.

Wakin, Edward. *Enter the Irish American.* New York: Thomas Y. Crowell, 1976.

Wall, Maryjean. *How Kentucky Became Southern: A Tale of Outlaws, Horse Thieves, Gamblers, and Breeders.* Lexington: University Press of Kentucky, 2010.

Bibliography

Waller, George. *Saratoga: Saga of an Impious Era.* New York: Bonanza Books, 1966.

Werner, M. R. *Tammany Hall.* Garden City, N.J.: Doubleday, Doran and Company, 1928.

Wingate, Charles F. "An Episode in Municipal Government: The Reign of the Ring." *North American Review,* January 1875.

Index

CPSIA information can be obtained at www.ICGtesting.com
Printed in the USA
BVOW08*1728270316

441725BV00001B/1/P